ON

TOUCHSTONE

STUDENT'S BOOK 2B

MICHAEL MCCARTHY
JEANNE MCCARTEN
HELEN SANDIFORD

CAMBRIDGE
UNIVERSITY PRESS

T0303277

CAMBRIDGE
UNIVERSITY PRESS & ASSESSMENT

Shaftesbury Road, Cambridge CB2 8EA, United Kingdom

One Liberty Plaza, 20th Floor, New York, NY 10006, USA

477 Williamstown Road, Port Melbourne, VIC 3207, Australia

314–321, 3rd Floor, Plot 3, Splendor Forum, Jasola District Centre, New Delhi – 110025, India

103 Penang Road, #05–06/07, Visioncrest Commercial, Singapore 238467

Cambridge University Press & Assessment is a department of the University of Cambridge.

We share the University's mission to contribute to society through the pursuit of education, learning and research at the highest international levels of excellence.

www.cambridge.org
Information on this title: www.cambridge.org/9781107627048

© Cambridge University Press & Assessment 2005, 2014

This publication is in copyright. Subject to statutory exception and to the provisions of relevant collective licensing agreements, no reproduction of any part may take place without the written permission of Cambridge University Press & Assessment.

First published 2005
Second edition 2014

20 19 18

Printed in Mexico by Litográfica Ingramex, S.A. de C.V.

A catalogue record for this publication is available from the British Library

ISBN 978-1-107-68173-6 Student's Book
ISBN 978-1-107-68175-0 Student's Book A
ISBN 978-1-107-62704-8 Student's Book B
ISBN 978-1-107-69037-0 Workbook
ISBN 978-1-107-64988-0 Workbook A
ISBN 978-1-107-61861-9 Workbook B
ISBN 978-1-107-65940-7 Full Contact
ISBN 978-1-107-61439-0 Full Contact A
ISBN 978-1-107-66547-7 Full Contact B
ISBN 978-1-107-62402-3 Teacher's Edition with Assessment Audio CD/CD-ROM
ISBN 978-1-107-67757-9 Class Audio CDs (4)

Additional resources for this publication at www.cambridge.org/touchstone2

Cambridge University Press & Assessment has no responsibility for the persistence or accuracy of URLs for external or third-party internet websites referred to in this publication, and does not guarantee that any content on such websites is, or will remain, accurate or appropriate. Information regarding prices, travel timetables, and other factual information given in this work is correct at the time of first printing but Cambridge University Press & Assessment does not guarantee the accuracy of such information thereafter.

Acknowledgments

***Touchstone Second Edition* has benefited from extensive development research. The authors and publishers would like to extend their thanks to the following reviewers and consultants for their valuable insights and suggestions:**

Ana Lúcia da Costa Maia de Almeida and Mônica da Costa Monteiro de Souza from **IBEU**, Rio de Janeiro, Brazil; Andreza Cristiane Melo do Lago from **Magic English School,** Manaus, Brazil; Magaly Mendes Lemos from **ICBEU**, São José dos Campos, Brazil; Maria Lucia Zaorob, São Paulo, Brazil; Patricia McKay Aronis from **CEL LEP**, São Paulo, Brazil; Carlos Gontow, São Paulo, Brazil; Christiane Augusto Gomes da Silva from **Colégio Visconde de Porto Seguro,** São Paulo, Brazil; Silvana Fontana from **Lord's Idiomas**, São Paulo, Brazil; Alexander Fabiano Morishigue from **Speed Up Idiomas**, Jales, Brazil; Elisabeth Blom from **Casa Thomas Jefferson**, Brasília, Brazil; Michelle Dear from **International Academy of English**, Toronto, ON, Canada; Walter Duarte Marin, Laura Hurtado Portela, Jorge Quiroga, and Ricardo Suarez, from **Centro Colombo Americano**, Bogotá, Colombia; Jhon Jairo Castaneda Macias from **Praxis English Academy**, Bucaramanga, Colombia; Gloria Liliana Moreno Vizcaino from **Universidad Santo Tomas**, Bogotá, Colombia; Elizabeth Ortiz from **Copol English Institute (COPEI),** Guayaquil, Ecuador; Henry Foster from **Kyoto Tachibana University,** Kyoto, Japan; Steven Kirk from **Tokyo University**, Tokyo, Japan; J. Lake from **Fukuoka Woman's University**, Fukuoka, Japan; Etsuko Yoshida from **Mie University**, Mie, Japan; B. Bricklin Zeff from **Hokkai Gakuen University**, Hokkaido, Japan; Ziad Abu-Hamatteh from **Al-Balqa' Applied University**, Al-Salt, Jordan; Roxana Pérez Flores from **Universidad Autonoma de Coahuila Language Center**, Saltillo, Mexico; Kim Alejandro Soriano Jimenez from **Universidad Politecnica de Altamira**, Altamira, Mexico; Tere Calderon Rosas from **Universidad Autonoma Metropolitana Campus Iztapalapa**, Mexico City, Mexico; Lilia Bondareva, Polina Ermakova, and Elena Frumina, from **National Research Technical University MISiS**, Moscow, Russia; Dianne C. Ellis from **Kyung Hee University**, Gyeonggi-do, South Korea; Jason M. Ham and Victoria Jo from **Institute of Foreign Language Education, Catholic University of Korea**, Gyeonggi-do, South Korea; Shaun Manning from **Hankuk University of Foreign Studies**, Seoul, South Korea; Natalie Renton from **Busan National University of Education**, Busan, South Korea; Chris Soutter from **Busan University of Foreign Studies**, Busan, South Korea; Andrew Cook from **Dong A University**, Busan, South Korea; Raymond Wowk from **Daejin University**, Gyeonggi-do, South Korea; Ming-Hui Hsieh and Jessie Huang from **National Central University**, Zhongli, Taiwan; Kim Phillips from **Chinese Culture University**, Taipei, Taiwan; Alex Shih from **China University of Technology**, Taipei Ta-Liao Township, Taiwan; Porntip Bodeepongse from **Thaksin University**, Songkhla, Thailand; Nattaya Puakpong and Pannathon Sangarun from **Suranaree University of Technology**, Nakhon Ratchasima, Thailand; Barbara Richards, Gloria Stewner-Manzanares, and Caroline Thompson, from **Montgomery College**, Rockville, MD, USA; Kerry Vrabel from **Gateway Community College**, Phoenix, AZ, USA.

Touchstone Second Edition* authors and publishers would also like to thank the following individuals and institutions who have provided excellent feedback and support on *Touchstone Blended:

Gordon Lewis, Vice President, Laureate Languages and Chris Johnson, Director, Laureate English Programs, Latin America from **Laureate International Universities**; **Universidad de las Americas**, Santiago, Chile; **University of Victoria**, Paris, France; **Universidad Technólogica Centroamericana**, Honduras; **Instititut Universitaire de Casablanca**, Morocco; **Universidad Peruana de Ciencias Aplicadas**, Lima, Peru; **CIBERTEC**, Peru; **National Research Technical University (MiSIS)**, Moscow, Russia; **Institut Obert de Catalunya (IOC)**, Barcelona, Spain; Sedat Çilingir, Burcu Tezcan, and Didem Mutçalıoğlu from **İstanbul Bilgi Üniversitesi**, Istanbul, Turkey.

Touchstone Second Edition* authors and publishers would also like to thank the following contributors to *Touchstone Second Edition:

Sue Aldcorn, Frances Amrani, Deborah Gordon, Lisa Hutchins, Nancy Jordan, Steven Kirk, Genevieve Kocienda, Linda-Marie Koza, Geraldine Mark, Julianna Nielsen, Kathryn O'Dell, Nicola Prentis, Ellen Shaw, Kristin Sherman, Luis Silva Susa, Mary Vaughn, Kerry S. Vrabel, Shari Young, and Eric Zuarino.

Authors' Acknowledgments

The authors would like to thank all the Cambridge University Press staff and freelancers who were involved in the creation of *Touchstone Second Edition*. In addition, they would like to acknowledge a huge debt of gratitude that they owe to two people: Mary Vaughn, for her role in creating *Touchstone First Edition* and for being a constant source of wisdom ever since, and Bryan Fletcher, who also had the vision that has led to the success of *Touchstone Blended Learning*.

Helen Sandiford would like to thank her family for their love and support, especially her husband Bryan.

The author team would also like to thank each other, for the joy of working together, sharing the same professional dedication, and for the mutual support and friendship.

Finally, the authors would like to thank our dear friend Alejandro Martinez, Global Training Manager, who sadly passed away in 2012. He is greatly missed by all who had the pleasure to work with him. Alex was a huge supporter of *Touchstone* and everyone is deeply grateful to him for his contribution to its success.

Touchstone Level 2B Contents and learning outcomes

Interaction	Skills				Self study
Conversation strategies	Listening	Reading	Writing	Free talk	Vocabulary notebook
• Respond to suggestions • Use *I guess* when you're not sure	***It's good to travel.*** • Predict what people are going to say about traveling, then listen for the exact words ***Recommendations*** • Match advice about staying at hotels with pictures, then listen to a radio show to check your answers	***Unique hotel experiences*** • Read an article about three unusual hotels	***Recommendations*** • Write an email about staying at one of the hotels in the lesson • Format and expressions for writing an email	***Travel smart!*** • Role play: Choose a role and give your partner travel advice according to the pictures	***Travel items*** • When you write down a new noun, write notes about it
• Ask politely for permission to do things with *Do you mind . . . ?* • Ask someone politely to do something with *Would you mind . . . ?* • Agree to requests	***Could you do me a favor?*** • Listen to conversations between roommates, complete their requests, and then check if each person agrees ***Evening routines*** • Listen to someone describe his evening routine, and number pictures in order	***Do you have an unusual home habit?*** • Read online comments about people's unusual home habits	***Evening routines*** • Write a short article about the evening routines of your partner • Order events using sequence words	***All about home*** • Pair work: Discuss questions about your homes, and find out ways you are alike and different	***The ABCs of home*** • Write down a word for something in your home for each letter of the alphabet
• React to and comment on a story • Respond with *I bet . . .*	***A funny story*** • Listen to an anecdote, and choose the best response ***Happy endings?*** • Listen to two anecdotes, and answer questions about the details	***Every cloud has a silver lining . . .*** • Read a magazine article featuring anecdotes from readers	***Anecdotes*** • Write an anecdote telling about a time something went wrong • Link ideas with *when* and *while*	***What was happening?*** • Pair work: Look at a picture, and see how much detail you can remember about what was happening	***From head to toe*** • Draw and label pictures to remember new vocabulary
Checkpoint Units 7–9 pages 95–96					
• Interrupt and restart phone conversations • Use *just* to soften things you say	***Sorry about that!*** • Listen to three phone conversations to infer the reason for each call and for each interruption ***It can be annoying . . .*** • Listen to a teenager talk about texting; check the opinions she agrees with	***Why all the interest in texting?*** • Read an online article about texting	***The pros and cons*** • Write a short article about the advantages and disadvantages of a means of communication • Structure of an article comparing pros and cons	***Which is better?*** • Pair work: Compare pairs of actions, and discuss which is better and why	***Phone talk*** • Learn new expressions by making note of the situations when you can use them
• Show you're trying to remember a word or name • Use *You mean . . .* or *Do you mean . . .?* to help someone remember something	***Celebrities*** • Listen to descriptions of celebrities, and match them with their photos ***What's in style?*** • Listen to four people answer questions about current styles, and fill in a chart	***Fashion statements*** • Read a blog article about fashion trends	***Fashion trends*** • Write a fashion article describing the current "look" • Expressions to describe new and old trends	***What's different?*** • Pair work: Ask and answer questions to determine what's different about people in two pictures, and guess where they went	***What do they look like?*** • Use new vocabulary in true sentences about yourself or people you know
• Make offers and promises with *I'll* and *I won't* • Agree to something with *All right* and *OK*	***I'll do it!*** • Listen to two people planning a party, and identify what each of them says they'll do ***A good idea?*** • Listen to two people discussing predictions; identify who says each is a good idea and why	***What will life be like in the future?*** • Read an online article with predictions about the future	***A good idea?*** • Write a short article about how a future invention will make our lives better or worse • List ideas with *First*, *Second*, *Next*, and *Finally*	***I might do that.*** • Pair work: Interview a classmate to find out his or her future plans	***Writers, actors, and artists*** • Write new vocabulary in groups by endings or topics
Checkpoint Units 10–12 pages 127–128					

Useful language for . . .

Getting help

How do you say "__________" in English?

I'm sorry. What did you say?

How do you say this word?

What do we have to do?

I don't understand. What do you mean?

Do you mean __________?

Can you spell "__________" for me, please?

Working with a partner

Whose turn is it now?

It's my / your turn.

Do you want to go first?

OK. I'll go first. / No, you go first.

This time we change roles.

OK. I'll start.

Are we done?

Yes, I think so. Let's try it again.

Let's compare answers.

OK. What do you have for number 1?

Do you have __________ for number 3?

No, I have __________. Let's check again.

Do you understand this sentence?

Yeah. It means "__________."

UNIT 7

Going away

Can Do! In this unit, you learn how to . . .

Lesson A
- Talk about getting ready for a trip using infinitives to give reasons
- Give opinions using *It's* + adjective + *to*

Lesson B
- Talk about things to take on a trip
- Give advice and suggestions with *should, could, need to,* etc.

Lesson C
- Respond to suggestions
- Use *I guess* when you're not sure

Lesson D
- Read an article about unique hotels
- Write an email about a trip

1

2

3

4

Before you begin . . .

Brainstorm! Think of three . . .

- fun places to go on a trip.
- things you always take on a trip.
- fun things to do on a trip.
- different ways to travel.

Lesson A Getting ready

Alicia So, are you all packed for your trip?
Rita No. I'm nowhere near ready – look at my to-do list! I need to go shopping to get a suitcase. And I still have to go online to find a flight.
Alicia Uh-oh. So, is it expensive to fly to Puerto Rico – or is it easy to find cheap flights?
Rita Well, it's not *too* hard to find a bargain. You just have to do some research.
Alicia Right. So why are you going exactly?
Rita To see my relatives in San Juan. Then we're all going someplace to go snorkeling.
Alicia Nice. Sounds like a fun trip. Good luck with your list.
Rita Thanks.

1 Getting started

A **Look at Rita's "to-do" list for her upcoming trip. What other things do you need to do before a trip? Make a class list.**

B 3.01 **Listen. What's Rita going to do in Puerto Rico? Is she ready for the trip? Practice the conversation.**

Figure it out **C** **Circle the correct verb forms to complete the sentences. Use the conversation above to help you.**

1. I'm going to Puerto Rico **see** / **to see** my relatives.
2. I still have to go online **to buy** / **buying** a ticket.
3. **Is it** / **Is** cheap to fly to Puerto Rico?
4. **Is** / **It's** easy to find a bargain.

2 Grammar Infinitives for reasons; *It's* + adjective + *to* . . . 3.02

Extra practice p. 146

You can use an infinitive to give a reason.

Why are you going to Puerto Rico?
To see my relatives.
I'm going to Puerto Rico **to see** my relatives.
I need to go shopping **to get** a suitcase.
I have to go online **to find** a flight.

You can use *It's* + adjective + *to* to describe a verb.

Is it expensive **to fly**? (NOT ~~Is expensive to fly?~~)
It's easy **to find** a cheap flight online. (NOT ~~Is easy . . .~~)
Is it easy **to find** bargains online?
It's easy **to do**.
It's not hard **to do.**

In conversation

The top five adjectives in the structure ***It's*** ______ ***to*** . . . are ***hard, nice, easy, good,*** and ***important***.

A Complete the conversation extracts. Use infinitives for reasons and *it's* / *is it* + adjective + *to*. Then practice with a partner.

1. A I'm going to *go to Tokyo to study Japanese* (go to Tokyo / study Japanese) next month. I'm staying with a family on an exchange program. I just got my visa.
   B Wow! So, ____________________ (necessary / learn some Japanese) before you go?
   A Well, yeah. ____________________ (nice / say "Thank you") and things. ____________________ (important / know a few expressions) I think, so I want to ____________________ (get a phrase book / read) on the plane.

2. A I need to ____________________ (buy a guidebook / get some ideas) for sightseeing, too.
   B So, ____________________ (easy / get around) Tokyo?
   A Well, they say ____________________ (not hard / use the subway). But I heard ____________________ (easy / get lost) when you're walking around.

3. A I need to ____________________ (go to the bank / change some money), too. I heard ____________________ (good / have some cash). You know, you need to ____________________ (carry some cash / pay for taxis) and things.
   B ____________________ (not possible / pay) for everything with a credit card?
   A Not really. ____________________ (not easy / do) that.

B Pair work Choose a country to visit. Role-play a conversation about preparing for the trip. Use the conversation above for ideas. Think of more questions to ask.

*A **I'd love to go to Brazil to see the Carnival in Rio.***
*B **Is it expensive to fly there?***

3 Speaking naturally Reduction of *to*

A *Is it expensive **to** visit your country?*   B *Well, it's hard **to** find cheap hotels.*

A 3.03 Listen and repeat. Notice the reduction of *to* in the sentences above.

About you **B 3.04 Listen and complete the questions. Then ask and answer the questions with a partner.**

1. Do you need a visa ____________ your country?
2. Do you need to speak the language ____________ your city?
3. Is it easy ____________ a cheap place to stay?
4. Is it safe ____________ late at night?
5. Do you have to pay ____________ in museums?

1 Building vocabulary

A 3.05 Listen and say the words. What else do you see in the picture? Make a list. Can you think of any other things you need when you travel? Compare with a partner.

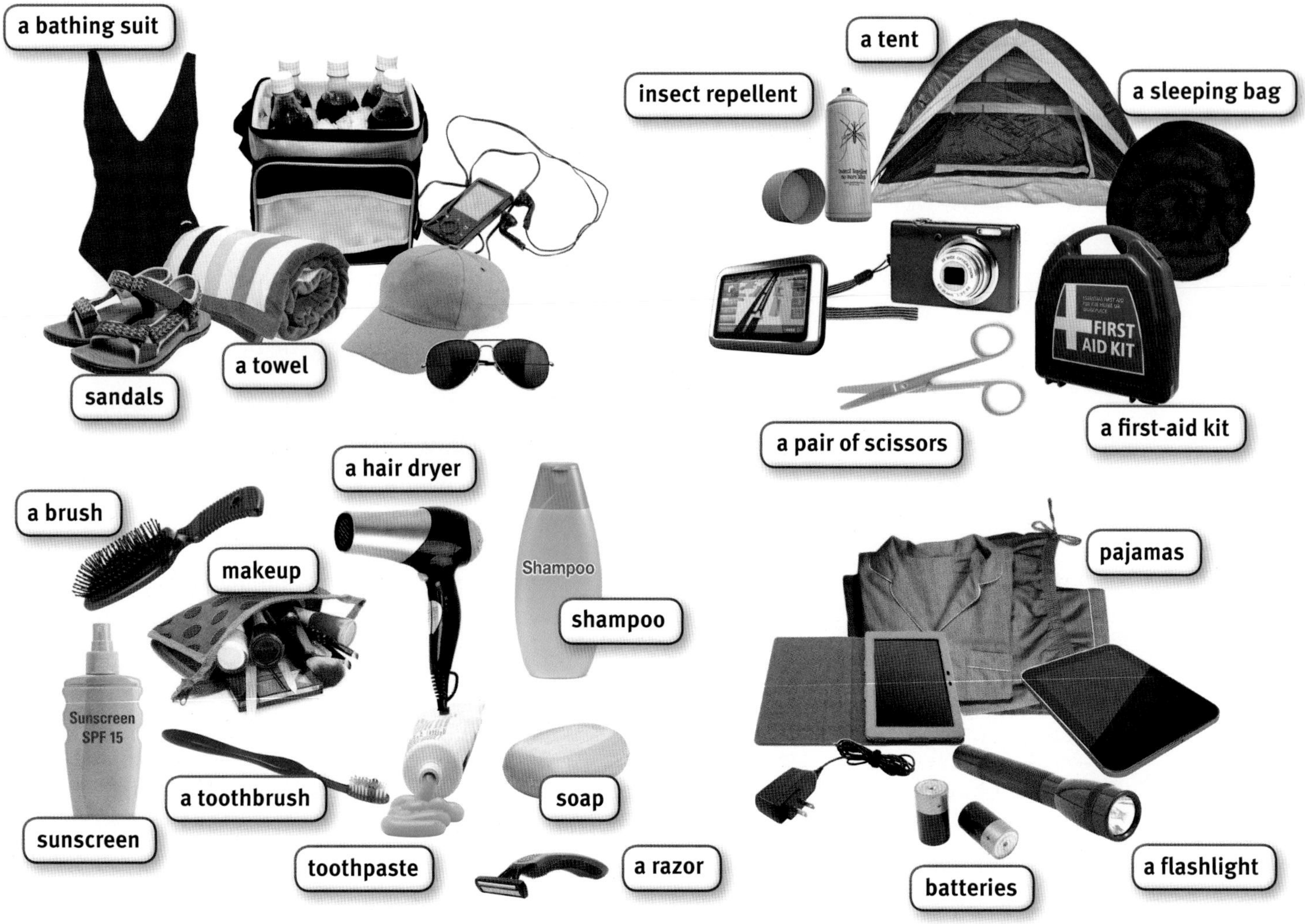

Word sort **B** Complete the chart using at least 15 different words. Then compare with a partner.

	You need to take . . .	It's good to have . . .	It's not necessary to take . . .
On a beach vacation	*a bathing suit*	*sunscreen*	*a tent*
On a camping trip			
To stay overnight with a friend			

"On a beach vacation, you need to take a bathing suit to go swimming."

Vocabulary notebook p. 74

2 Building language

A 3.06 **Listen. Jenny's going on a camping trip. What's her mother's advice? Practice the conversation.**

Mom Jenny, maybe you should take some insect repellent. . . . Oh, and take a flashlight, and don't forget to pack some spare batteries. . . . Why don't you take my jacket? It's a good idea to have something warm. . . . Now, you need to take a hat. You could borrow your dad's. But don't lose it. . . . Oh, and Jenny, do you want to pack some other shoes?

Jenny I'm sorry, Mom. Did you say something? I can't hear you with my headphones on.

Figure it out **B** **How does Jenny's mother make suggestions? What does she say about packing these things?**

insect repellent | a flashlight | spare batteries | her jacket | something warm | a hat | other shoes

"You should take some insect repellent."

3 Grammar Advice and suggestions 3.07

Extra practice p. 146

What **should** I take?
Should I take these shoes?
You **should** take a hat.
You **shouldn't** take high heels.
You **could** borrow your dad's hat.
You **need to** have warm clothes.

Do you want to pack some other shoes?
Why don't you take a hat?
It's a good idea to pack a jacket.
Take a flashlight.
Don't forget to pack some batteries.

In conversation

You should . . . can be very strong. People sometimes soften it by saying:
I think you should . . .
Maybe you should (just) . . .
You should probably . . .

A **Complete the suggestions to someone going on these trips. Then compare with a partner. Add more suggestions.**

1. **a hiking trip in the Andes**
"I think you should ___*take a first-aid kit*___."
"It's a good idea ________________."
"Maybe you shouldn't ________________."

2. **sightseeing in Paris**
"Don't forget ________________."
"Why don't you ________________?"
"Maybe you should ________________."

3. **a language course in Canada**
"You need ________________."
"It's not a good idea ________________."
"You could ________________."

4. **backpacking around Asia**
"Take ________________."
"You should probably ________________."
"You want to ________________."

About you **B** **Pair work** **Now look at these trip ideas. Make four suggestions to someone going on these trips.**

Why don't you take some souvenirs to your relatives in the U.S.?

- visiting relatives in the U.S.
- a homestay in Japan
- a working vacation in Australia
- a road trip through California

Common errors

Do not use *can* to give advice.
I think you **should** *take a first-aid kit.*
(NOT *I think you* ~~*can*~~ *take a first-aid kit.*)

Sounds right p. 138

That's a great idea.

1 Conversation strategy Responding to suggestions

A **Would you like to take a few days off and go away? What would you do? Tell the class.**

B 3.08 **Listen. What would Chris and Stan like to do? What are they probably going to do?**

Chris You know, we should take a few days off sometime.

Stan Yeah, we should. Definitely.

Chris We could go to Mexico or something.

Stan That's a great idea.

Chris We could even go for a couple of weeks.

Stan Well, maybe. I guess we could, but . . .

Chris You know, we could just quit our jobs and maybe go backpacking for a few months. . . .

Stan Well, I don't know. I'd like to, but . . . I guess I need to keep this job, you know, to pay for school and stuff.

Chris Yeah, me too, I guess.

C **Notice how Stan responds to Chris's suggestions with expressions like these. Find examples in the conversation.**

For suggestions you like:
That's a great idea.
That sounds great.
I'd love to.

For suggestions you don't like:
Maybe.
I guess we could, but . . .
I don't know.
I'd like to, but . . .

D **Complete each response with an appropriate expression. Use six different expressions. Then practice with a partner.**

1. A Why don't we take a beach vacation soon?
   B ____________ We can go windsurfing!
2. A You should ski with me this weekend.
   B ____________ I have to work.
3. A Why don't we go to Boston next month?
   B ____________ I don't have any money.
4. A Let's go camping this weekend.
   B ____________ I think it's going to rain.
5. A We could go to Moscow in February.
   B ____________ It's really cold in February.
6. A Let's go to New Zealand for a vacation.
   B ____________ New Zealand is beautiful!

About you **E** **Pair work** **Practice again. Use your own responses and continue each conversation. Can you agree on something you'd both like to do?**

2 Strategy plus *I guess*

You can use *I guess* when you're not 100% sure about something or if you don't want to sound 100% sure.

In conversation

I guess is one of the top 20 expressions.

3.09 Check (✓) where you think the speakers say *I guess*. Then listen and write *I guess* where you hear it. Practice with a partner.

1. A I really prefer warm weather to cold. How about you ________ ?
   B ✓ *I guess* I like cold weather more. It's a lot of fun to do winter sports ________ .
   A That's true ________ . You can go sledding and stuff. We should ________ do that sometime!

2. A So, what's your idea of a good vacation?
   B Well, I kind of like to go camping. ________ that's my favorite thing to do.
   A Really ________ ? That sounds like fun. Hey, why don't we go together sometime ________ ?
   B Yeah. ________ we could go next summer, maybe.

3 Listening and strategies It's good to travel.

A 3.10 Pair work Guess the missing words. Then listen to conversations between Mark and his friends. Write the missing words.

1. You have to ____________ a country to really understand its culture.
2. It's important to ____________ when you travel.
3. It's good to ____________ tourist areas when you go somewhere.
4. It's not possible to ____________ in a short trip.
5. You should try ____________ when you go to a new place.

B 3.10 Listen again. Circle the correct words to complete Mark's suggestions (A) below. Complete his friends' responses (B) with two words.

1. A Let's go to **Mexico** / **Miami** this summer.
   B I'd like to, but is it easy to find ________ ________ ?
2. A Why don't we go to a **French** / **Italian** class?
   B I guess we could, but I really want to ________ ________ .
3. A We could **drive** / **hike** along the coast sometime.
   B That sounds great. Are there any ________ ________ to stay?
4. A We should go **scuba diving** / **backpacking** in Australia.
   B I don't know. It's not easy to go. I have ________ ________ .
5. A Do you want to go to a Chinese **exhibition** / **festival**?
   B I'd love to! Do they have ________ and ________ and everything?

About you **C Class activity** **Make the suggestions above to six classmates. How many say yes?**

1 Reading

A Brainstorm! Do you ever stay in hotels? What's fun about staying in a hotel? Make a class list.

You don't have to cook or make your bed.
You can sit by the pool to relax.

Reading tip

If you don't understand some words in a description, find other words that will help you get a sense of their meaning. For example, *comfortable* helps you know that *cozy* means "nice in some way."

B Read the article as quickly as you can. How much can you remember about each hotel? Compare with a partner.

Unique Hotel Experiences

Here are three exciting hotels that you will never forget!

1. Controversy Tram Hotel, The Netherlands It's easy to see why this bed and breakfast is on our list of unusual places to stay. Don't worry – these old city trams are not going to take you anywhere. The owners got old trams from Germany and Holland and converted them into comfortable, cozy rooms with American, Italian, French, and Mexican themes. The owners sleep in an old double-decker bus from England and cook in a French van! It's definitely a place for people who like trains, planes, cars, and other transportation memorabilia.

2. EcoCamp, Chile It's not hard to fall asleep at this environmentally friendly hotel in the heart of the Torres del Paine National Park. The scenery is amazing, as is the peace and quiet. Guests stay in comfortable and inviting domes similar to the homes of ancient native peoples. You should definitely take your hiking boots. In the daytime, guests can trek through the mountains and see *guanacos* (a type of llama) and other wildlife and then go back to the domes to relax and enjoy a delicious dinner in the evening.

3. Giraffe Manor, Nairobi When we asked the owners of this African hotel, "What should we pack?" they said, "Don't forget to bring a camera." It's good to know. From the elegant rooms of this beautiful manor you have superb views of the Ngong Hills. Not only that, but a herd of giraffes lives on the manor, and you don't have to try hard to get a great photo. The giraffes wander around and poke their heads through the bedroom windows. They even turn up at the breakfast table, too.

C Pair work Read the article again. Discuss the questions about each hotel.

1. What is unusual about each hotel?
2. How does the article describe the rooms?
3. What can you do during the day in each place?
4. Which hotel would you like to stay at? Why?

2 Listening and writing Recommendations

A Look at these hotels. Would you like to visit any of them?

1

The Cave Hotel

2

The Lighthouse Hotel

3

The Spa Hotel

B 3.11 Read the advice about staying at these hotels. Can you match each piece of advice with a hotel? Then listen and check your guesses.

1. You should bring lots of books and board games for rainy days. __2__
2. Wear flat shoes so you can climb the ladder to your room. _____
3. Be sure to take everything you need. It's miles from another town. _____
4. I really recommend the hot-air balloon ride. _____
5. Don't spend too much time in the water. _____
6. It's a good idea to have some binoculars to watch the dolphins. _____

About you **C Imagine you are staying at one of the hotels in this lesson. Write an email to a classmate about the hotel and your trip. Use the Help note and the example below to help you.**

Help note

Writing a message about a trip

Start like this: ▶
Say if you are enjoying your stay: ▶
Describe the place, food, or weather: ▶
Say something you did: ▶
Attach a photo and describe it: ▶
Say something you are going to do: ▶
End like this: ▶

D Pair work Exchange messages. Write a response to your partner's message. Make comments and ask questions for more information.

Free talk p. 132

Vocabulary notebook Travel items

Learning tip *Writing notes about nouns*

When you write down a new noun, it's a good idea to write notes about it.

its pronunciation and stress ▶	*phrase book (ph = /f/)*
if it's a countable or an uncountable noun ▶	*sunscreen (uncountable)*
	a map (countable)
the spelling of the singular and plural forms ▶	*a hairbrush, hairbrushes*
if it's always plural ▶	*sunglasses (always plural)*
how to make a plural noun singular ▶	*a pair of sunglasses (singular)*

1 Match the travel items to the notes. Mark the stress on each word by underlining the stressed syllable.

1. bathing suit *d*
2. batteries ____
3. clothes ____
4. schedule ____
5. scissors ____

a. (*sc* = /s/), plural, *a pair of* (singular)
b. (sounds almost like *close*), always plural
c. (*sch* = /sk/), countable
d. (*ui* in *suit* sounds like *oo* in *too*), countable
e. ies = y (*singular*)

In conversation

A pair of shoes

The top items people talk about with ***a pair of*** are:

1. shoes
2. pants
3. shorts
4. jeans
5. glasses
6. stockings
7. socks
8. gloves

2 Write notes about these travel items. Add two more ideas of your own.

pajamas razor shampoo toothbrush

On your own

Visit some travel websites and find two different types of vacations. List ten items you need for each one.

Can Do! Now I can . . .

✓ I can . . . ? I need to review how to . . .

- ☐ give reasons for things I do.
- ☐ give opinions with *It's* + adjective + *to*.
- ☐ discuss what I need to take on a trip.
- ☐ give advice and make suggestions.
- ☐ respond to suggestions people make.
- ☐ use *I guess* to show I'm not sure about something.
- ☐ understand conversations about travel.
- ☐ understand advice people give about hotels.
- ☐ read an article about unique hotels.
- ☐ write an email about a trip.

UNIT 8

At home

Can Do! In this unit, you learn how to . . .

Lesson A
- Talk about where you keep things at home
- Say who owns things with *mine*, *yours*, etc. and *whose*

Lesson B
- Talk about items in the home
- Identify things using adjectives and *one* and *ones*

Lesson C
- Use *Do you mind . . . ?* and *Would you mind . . . ?* to make polite requests
- Agree to requests with expressions like *Go right ahead* and *No problem*

Lesson D
- Read comments on a website about unusual habits
- Write about your evening routine with expressions like *first* and *as soon as*

Before you begin . . .

Look at the pictures. What do you keep in these places?

Are you a pack rat – do you hate to throw things away?

Lesson A Spring cleaning

John	There's so much stuff in here! Are all these things really ours? I mean, whose bathing suit is this? Is it yours or your grandmother's?
Sandra	Hey, it's mine, and I like it.
John	And whose clothes are these?
Sandra	Oh, they're my sister's. She's storing some things here while she's away. The jewelry's hers, too. Ugh, look at these awful earrings. She has such weird taste.
John	But those are yours. I bought them for you!
Sandra	Oh, you did? Sorry. I guess they're not so bad.

1 Getting started

A **Look at the picture. What are John and Sandra doing? What's in their closet?**

B 3.12 **Listen. Who do the clothes belong to? the jewelry? Then practice the conversation.**

Figure it out **C** **Circle the correct words. Use the conversation above to help you. Then compare with a partner.**

1. A **Whose** / **Who's** bathing suit is this?
   B It's **my** / **mine**.
2. A **Who's** / **Whose** earrings are these? Are they **your** / **yours**?
   B No, they're my sister's. All the jewelry is **her** / **hers**.
3. A Does all this stuff belong to us?
   B Yes, it's all **our** / **ours**. They're all **our** / **ours** things.

2 Grammar *Whose . . . ?*; possessive pronouns 3.13

Extra practice p. 147

Whose bathing suit is this?
It's **mine**. (It's my bathing suit.)
Whose jewelry is this?
It's **hers**. (It's her jewelry.)
Whose clothes are these?
They're **ours**. (They're our clothes.)

It's **mine**.	It's my bathing suit.
They're **yours**.	They're your earrings.
It's **hers**.	It's her jewelry.
They're **his**.	They're his shoes.
They're **ours**.	They're our things.
It's **theirs**.	It's their stuff.

In conversation

20% of the uses of *mine* are in the expression *friend(s) of mine*.

About you **Complete the conversations with *whose* and possessive pronouns. Practice with a partner. Then practice again, giving your own answers.**

1. A I'm always losing my keys. Do you ever lose *yours* ?
   B No. We always keep _________ on a shelf next to the door.
2. A Do you hang your clothes in the closet every night?
   B Well, my sister always hangs _________ in the closet, but I just throw _________ on a chair! My room's always a mess.
3. A Where do you keep your shoes? Do you have one place?
   B No, they're all over the apartment. I have three brothers, and mom's always saying, " _________ shoes are these?"
4. A What do you do with your old clothes?
   B Sometimes I give things to a friend of _________ . But my parents give _________ to charity.
5. A Where do you put your cell phone at night?
   B I always leave _________ in the kitchen. But my husband puts _________ on the dresser. It's so annoying when it rings at night. So, what do you do with _________ ?
6. A What do you do with all of your photos?
   B I put family photos on my computer. But the kids keep _________ on their phones. My husband has _________ on his tablet.

3 Speaking naturally Grammatical words

A *Where **do you** keep **your** books?*
B ***On a** shelf **next to my** speakers. Where **do you** keep yours?*
A ***In a** pile **on the** floor **by my** bed.*

A 3.14 **Listen and repeat the conversation above. Notice how grammatical words like *do*, *you*, *your*, *on*, *a*, *next to*, *my*, *in*, and *by* are reduced. Only the content words are stressed.**

About you **B Pair work** **Make conversations like the one above. Use the ideas below or add your own.**

- jewelry
- headphones
- passport
- credit cards
- sports equipment
- music files

1 Building vocabulary

A 3.15 Listen and say the words. What else do you see in each picture? Make a list.

Word sort **B** Complete the chart with things in your home. Then compare with a partner.

Living room	Kitchen	My room	Other
sofa	*microwave*		

A In our living room, there's a sofa and . . .

B We don't have a sofa. We have a couple of armchairs and . . .

Vocabulary notebook p. 84

2 Building language

A 3.16 **Listen to these people shopping online. Which items does Meg like? Which items does Jon like? Do they have the same tastes?**

1

Jon: I need a new cover for my tablet. Which one do you like?
Meg: That nice black leather one there.
Jon: Hmm, I prefer the blue one in the middle.
Meg: Which one? The blue one with the orange dots? Really?
Jon: Yeah. It's really cool.

2

Jon: Oh, and I need some new speakers, too. Which ones do you like? The rectangular black ones?
Meg: Um, those cute little round ones are cool.
Jon: How about the orange ones on the right?
Meg: Hmm. Well, they go with the tablet cover, I guess.

Figure it out **B** **Pair work** **Choose the correct words. Then practice with a partner.**

A I like that **black nice** / **nice black** tablet cover.
B I like that blue **one** / **ones** in the middle.
A And do you like those cute **round little** / **little round** speakers?
B Which **one** / **ones**? The orange **one** / **ones**?

Common errors

Don't put an adjective after a noun.

I like the ***round*** *speakers.*
(NOT *I like the ~~speakers round~~*.)

3 Grammar Order of adjectives; pronouns *one* and *ones* 3.17

Extra practice p. 147

Usual adjective order
opinion, size, shape, color, nationality, material
They have a **beautiful black leather** cover.
I want those **cute little round** speakers.

I like the black cover. Which **one** do you like?
I like the blue **one** in the middle.
Those speakers are cool. Which **ones** do you like?
I like the silver **ones** on the left/right.

In conversation

People usually use just one or two adjectives before a noun.

About you **Complete the sentences so they are true for you. Then practice with a partner.**

1
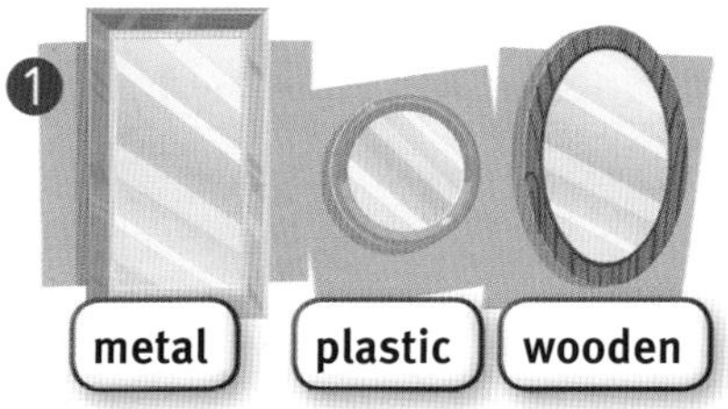

I don't like the ______________ .
Which _________ do you prefer?

2
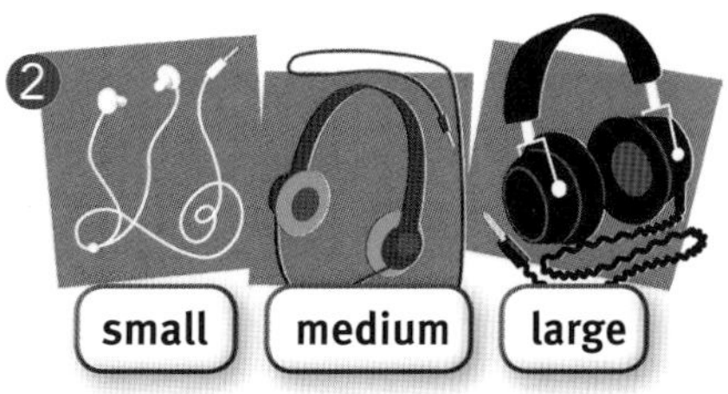

I like the ________________ .
Which _________ do you like?

3
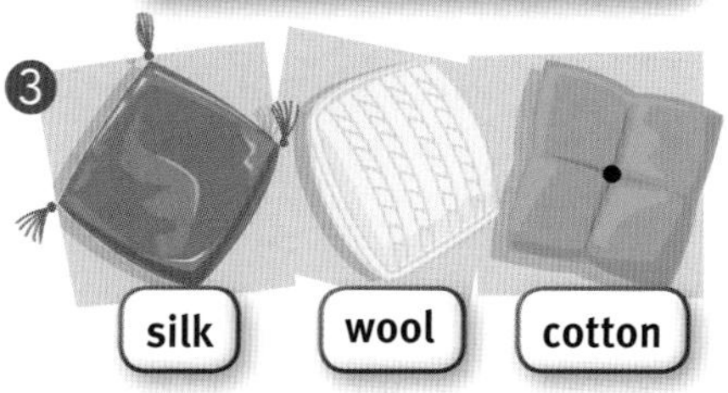

I'd like to have the ___________ .
Which _________ would you like?

A ***I like the big metal mirror. Which one do you like?***
B ***Well, I like the small pink one in the middle. The one with the plastic frame.***

Sounds right p. 138

Do you mind . . . ?

1 Conversation strategy Asking politely

A How can you make visitors to your home feel welcome when they arrive? What do you do or say?

B 3.18 Listen. What does Lucy ask permission to do? What request does Adam make?

Adam	Hi Lucy! Come on in.
Lucy	Thanks. I brought you some flowers. Are the others here yet?
Adam	No, not yet. So just make yourself at home. Thanks for these. Can I take your coat?
Lucy	Sure. Thanks. This is a great apartment. Do you mind if I look around?
Adam	No, go ahead.
Lucy	Oh, I love this antique table. It's beautiful.
Adam	Yeah, it's great, but it's not really mine. It's my mother's.
Lucy	Well, she has great taste.
Adam	Yeah. Listen, I hate to ask this, but I'm running a bit late. Would you mind helping me in the kitchen?
Lucy	No, not at all. What can I do?
Adam	Well, . . . could you chop the onions?
Lucy	No problem. I'm happy to help.

C Notice **how Lucy uses *Do you mind if. . . ?* to ask for permission, and Adam uses *Would you mind . . . -ing?* to ask Lucy to do something. Also notice that they answer "no" to show they agree. Find the examples in the conversation.**

"Do you mind if . . . ?"
"No, go ahead."
"Would you mind . . . -ing?"
"No, not at all."

D Pair work Imagine you are visiting your partner's home. Take turns asking permission to do these things and agreeing to the requests. Can you think of more ideas?

1. make a quick call
2. open a window
3. use your bathroom
4. take a cookie
5. get a glass of water
6. charge my phone

"Do you mind if I make a quick call?" *"No, go ahead."*

E Pair work Imagine your partner is visiting your home. Take turns asking him or her to do these things and agreeing to the requests. Can you think of more ideas?

1. answer the door for me
2. put this in the trash
3. set the table for me
4. make some coffee
5. help me with the dishes
6. turn on the oven

"Would you mind answering the door for me?" *"No, not at all."*

2 Strategy plus Agreeing to requests

Answer *Yes* to agree to requests with *Can* and *Could*:	**Answer *No* to agree to requests with *mind*:**
Can I look around?	*Do you mind if I look around?*
Yes. / Sure. / Go (right) ahead.	*No, go (right) ahead. / No, not at all.*
Could you chop the onions?	*Would you mind helping me in the kitchen?*
Yes. / Sure. / OK. / No problem.	*No, not at all. / Oh, no. No problem.*

In conversation

Do you mind __ing . . . ? and ***Would you mind if I . . . ?*** are possible but not very common.

3.19 Listen and complete the answers. Then practice with a partner.

1. A Do you mind if I sit here?
   B ____________________. Let me move my things.
2. A Could you do me a favor? Could you run to the store and get some milk?
   B ____________________. What kind of milk do you want?
3. A I forgot to charge my phone. Can I borrow yours for a minute?
   B ____________________. It's on the coffee table there.
4. A I think I left my wallet at home. Uh, would you mind lending me five dollars?
   B ____________________. Here, I have ten dollars.

3 Listening and strategies Could you do me a favor?

A 3.20 Listen to four conversations between roommates. What's the problem in each case?

1. ____________________
2. ____________________
3. ____________________
4. ____________________

B 3.21 Can you guess what favors each person is going to ask? Listen and complete the sentences. Do their roommates agree? Check (✓) the boxes.

	Agrees	Doesn't agree
1. Can you ____________________?	☐	☐
2. Would you mind ____________________?	☐	☐
3. Could you do me a favor? Could you ____________________?	☐	☐
4. Do you mind if I borrow ____________________?	☐	☐

C Class activity Ask your classmates for favors.

You want someone to . . .

- help install software on your laptop.
- find a phone number online for you.
- introduce you to their friend.

You need . . .

- to borrow some headphones.
- some money to buy some gum.
- help with some homework.

A ***Hey, Jen, would you mind helping me install some software on my computer?***
B ***Oh, I'm sorry. I'm not very good at computer stuff. I can't even do that on mine!***

Lesson D Home habits

1 Reading

A **Circle the words to make these statements true for you. Tell the class.**

- My kitchen is very **organized** / **disorganized**.
- I wash dishes **by hand** / **in the dishwasher**.
- I iron **none** / **some** / **all** of my clothes.
- I **save** / **throw out** used food containers.

B **Read the comments on the website. What habits do the people have? Which do you think are unusual?**

Reading tip

Ask yourself questions as you read, for example, *Is this logical? Is this normal?* etc.

http://www.personalhomestyle...

Do you have an unusual HOME HABIT?

view all | favorites | Post comment

Martin_442 March 31, 10:55 p.m. read full comment reply

Well, my best friend has a very disorganized kitchen, but you should see mine. As soon as I come back from grocery shopping, I organize everything. First, I arrange the cans so the vegetables are in one section and the canned fruit is in another section. Next, I sort them by size so the big ones are at the back and the small ones are at the front. Then I make sure I can see all the labels.

Charlotte April 21, 8:02 p.m. read full comment reply

We have a brand new expensive dishwasher, but I hate it. I don't think it washes very well. My friend says hers is great, but mine always leaves the glasses dirty. So I always wash the dishes by hand before I load them in the dishwasher. Then, after I take them out, I rinse them again to make sure they are clean! It drives my husband crazy!

Lucia_P April 22, 7:55 a.m. read full comment reply

My weird home habit? I iron everything, including my jeans, while I'm watching TV. I even iron my socks. My roommate just stuffs hers in a drawer, but I like to fold everything, too. I even iron the curtains in my bedroom every two weeks. I know it sounds crazy, but you iron yours, too, right?

Manas_No_more_chores April 22, 7:58 a.m. read full comment reply

OK, I can't help it. I save every small plastic take-out container, pizza box, cups from the coffee shop, salad cartons, etc. My friend just throws all his in the trash, but I think that's a waste. You can use them for a lot of different things. Like the big cardboard pizza boxes – we use ours during the summer for picnic trays.

C **Read the comments again. Answer the questions.**

1. How does Martin arrange the cans in his cupboards?
2. Why does Charlotte wash the dishes before she puts them in the dishwasher?
3. What does Lucia iron?
4. What does Manas do with the containers he saves?

About you **D** **Pair work** **What unusual habits does your family have? Tell your partner.**

2 Listening Evening routines

About you **A Do you do any of these things when you get home every day? Tell the class.**

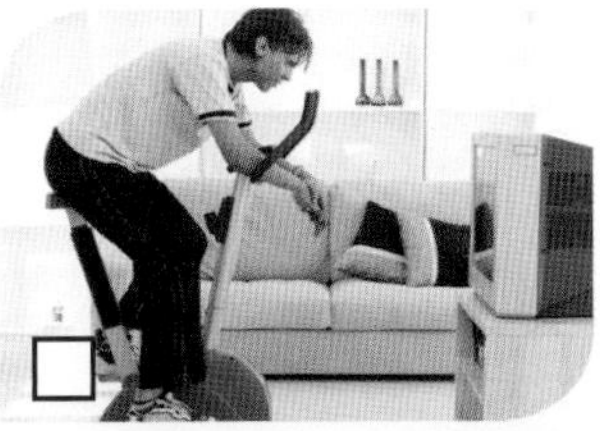

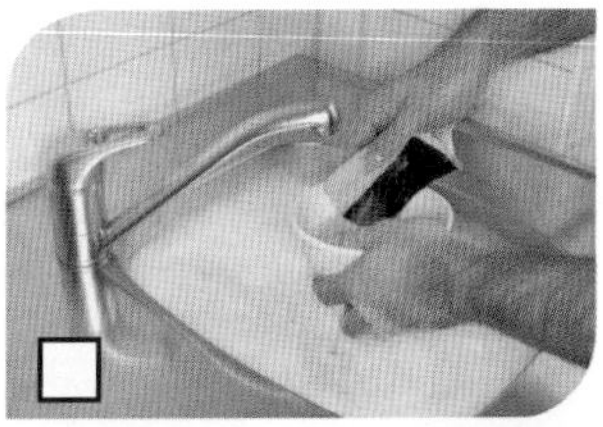

B 3.22 **Listen. What does Mike do when he gets home? Number the pictures in the correct order.**

C 3.22 **Listen again and answer the questions. Is your evening like Mike's?**

1. What does Mike take out of his pockets at night? Why?
2. When does he do the dishes? Why?
3. How does he feel after he exercises? After he watches the news?
4. What does he do just before he goes to sleep?

3 Speaking and writing Evening routines

About you **A Write answers to the questions below. Then ask and answer the questions with a partner. How are your routines the same?**

- What do you do as soon as you get home?
- What do you do before you have dinner?
- What do you do while you're eating?
- What's your bedtime routine?

About you **B Read the article below. Then write an article about your evening routine. Use the expressions in the Help note that order events.**

Home | Edit | Document Elements | Tables | Table Layout | Charts | Smart Art

My Evening Routines

First things first
As soon as I get home at night, I like to relax. **First**, I change my clothes. I put on something comfortable, like jeans and a T-shirt. **Next**, I turn on some music, **and then** I cook dinner. I like listening to music **while** I'm making dinner.

Dinnertime
I like to watch TV **during** dinner, so I eat in the living room. Right **after** dinner, I do the dishes. I hate to leave dirty dishes in the sink! **When** the kitchen is clean, I can relax.

Time for bed
I often have a snack **before** bedtime. **Then** I get my e-reader and go to bed. I read for about half an hour **before** I go to sleep.

Help note

Ordering events

- To show a sequence:
  first, next, (and) then
- Before a noun:
  before / after
  during = "at the same time as"
- To link actions:
  when
  as soon as = "immediately after," "right after"
  while = "at the same time as"
  before / after

Free talk p. 133

Learning tip *Alphabet game*

Make learning new words into a game! Choose a topic and try to think of a word for each letter of the alphabet.

1 Label the pictures. The first letter of each word is given for you.

a ______________

b ______________

c ______________

d ______________

2 Now complete your own alphabet chart. Can you think of something in your home for each letter?

a armchair	*h*	*o*	*v*
b	*i*	*p*	*w*
c	*j*	*q*	*x*
d	*k*	*r*	*y*
e	*l*	*s*	*z*
f	*m*	*t*	
g	*n*	*u*	

On your own

Make labels for different things in your home. Don't throw the label away until you can remember the new word.

Can Do! Now I can . . .

✓ I can . . . ? I need to review how to . . .

- ☐ talk about where I keep things at home.
- ☐ say who owns things.
- ☐ talk about furniture and home furnishings.
- ☐ identify and describe which things I mean.
- ☐ ask politely for permission to do things.
- ☐ ask other people to do things.
- ☐ agree to requests.
- ☐ understand requests for favors and replies.
- ☐ understand details about evening routines.
- ☐ read comments about unusual home habits.
- ☐ write about my evening routine.

UNIT 9

Things happen

Can Do! In this unit, you learn how to . . .

Lesson A
- Tell anecdotes about things that went wrong using the past continuous and simple past

Lesson B
- Talk about accidents (e.g., *I broke my arm.*) using the past continuous and *myself, yourself,* etc.

Lesson C
- React to show interest with expressions like *Oh, no!*
- Use *I bet* to show you're sure or that you understand

Lesson D
- Read anecdotes in an article
- Write an anecdote using *when* and *while*

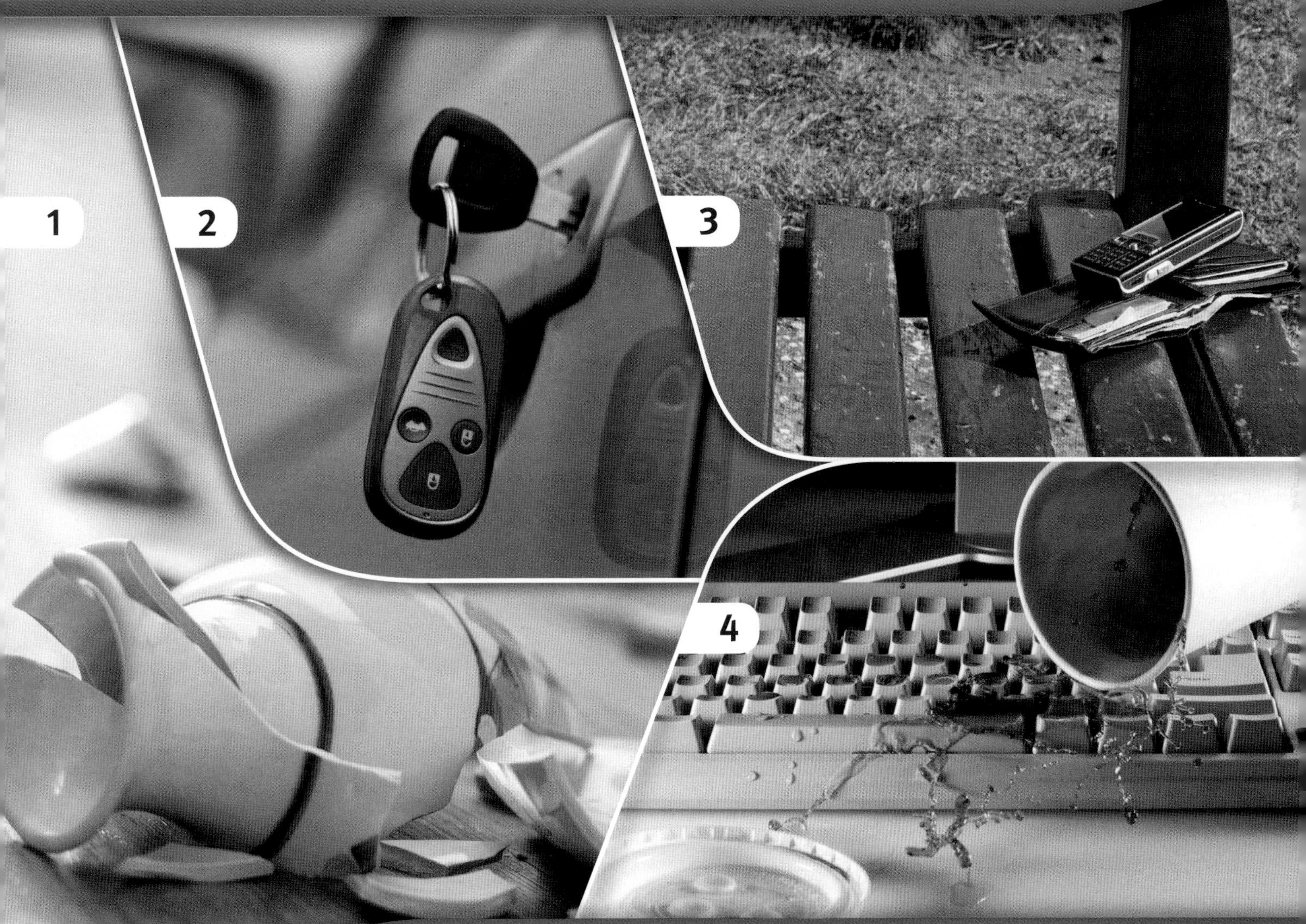

Before you begin . . .

Look at the pictures. Think about a time when one of these things happened to you. Tell the class about a time when you . . .

- broke something.
- forgot something.
- lost something.
- damaged something.

Are you having a BAD week?

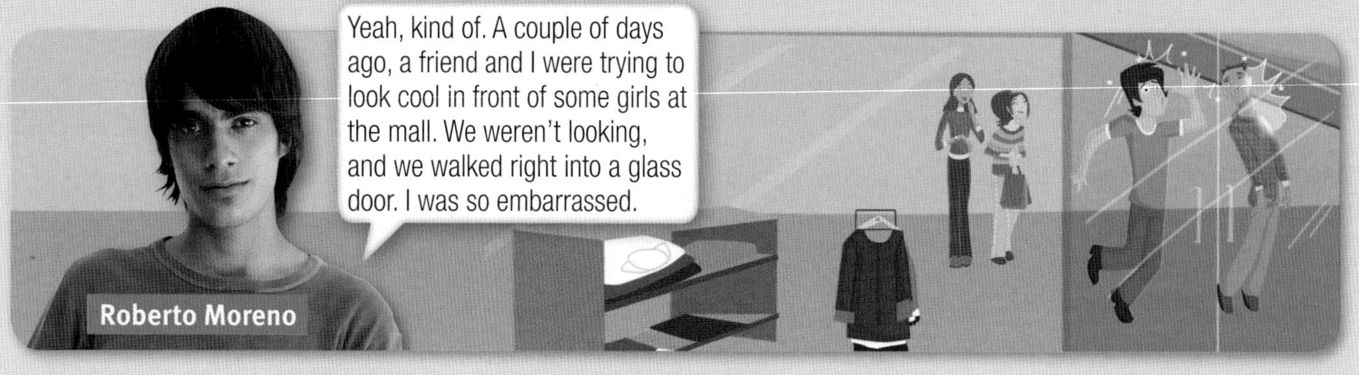

1 Getting started

A **Look at the illustrations above. What do you think happened to each person? Do these kinds of things ever happen to you? Tell the class.**

B 3.23 **Listen and read. Were your guesses about the people correct?**

Figure it out **C** **Can you choose the correct verb forms? Use the interviews above to help you. Then compare with a partner.**

1. Sean **missed / was missing** his stop because he **talked / was talking** to a woman on the train.
2. Julia's friend **deleted / was deleting** all Julia's music files when she **using / was using** her computer.
3. Roberto and his friend **tried / were trying** to look cool when they **walked / were walking** into a glass door.

2 Grammar Past continuous statements 3.24

Extra practice p. 148

Use the past continuous to set the background for a story or tell about events in progress in the past. Use the simple past for completed actions in the past.

I **was talking** to a woman, and I missed my stop. I **wasn't paying** attention.
We **were trying** to look cool, and we walked into a glass door. We **weren't looking**.
A friend of mine deleted all my music files **when** she **was using** my computer.
When my friend **was using** my computer, she deleted all my music files.

In conversation

The most common verbs in the past continuous are *talk*, *do*, *go*, *say*, *try*, *get*, and *tell*.

Complete the anecdotes with the past continuous or simple past. Then close your book. Take turns retelling the anecdotes to a partner.

1. I *was having* (have) lunch in a café yesterday when the server accidentally ______ (spill) tomato sauce on my shirt. I guess he ______ (not / pay) attention. I was upset, but I ______ (get) my lunch for free.
2. My friend and I were at a barbecue last week. When we ______ (walk) around the yard, she ______ (trip) and ______ (fall) into the pond.
3. I ______ (damage) my parents' car last week. I ______ (try) to park, and my friend ______ (talk) to me, and I ______ (hit) a wall. Now I have to pay for the repairs.
4. I was in a chemistry class recently, and a classmate and I ______ (do) an experiment when something ______ (go) wrong. I ______ (burn) my hand.
5. Last week I was on the bus, and I ______ (talk) to my girlfriend on my cell phone. Well, actually, we ______ (have) a long argument. We ______ (not / get along) at the time. When I ______ (end) the call, I realized that everyone on the bus ______ (listen). How embarrassing!

3 Speaking naturally Fall-rise intonation

I was running for a ***bus*** *last week, and I* ***fell****.*

When I was going ***home*** *yesterday, I ran into an old* ***friend****.*

A 3.25 **Listen and repeat the sentences above. Notice that the intonation falls and then rises slightly at the end of the first part of each sentence. This sets the background.**

B 3.26 **Listen and complete the sentences. Then listen again and repeat.**

1. I was reading a book ______, and I missed my stop.
2. Last night when I was washing ______, I broke a glass.
3. I was texting ______, and I tripped and fell on the street.
4. Yesterday when I was using ______, it suddenly crashed.

About you **C** **Pair work** Think of things that happened to you this week. Tell each other your anecdotes.

1 Building vocabulary

A 3.27 Listen and say the words and sentences. Which words and expressions do you already know?

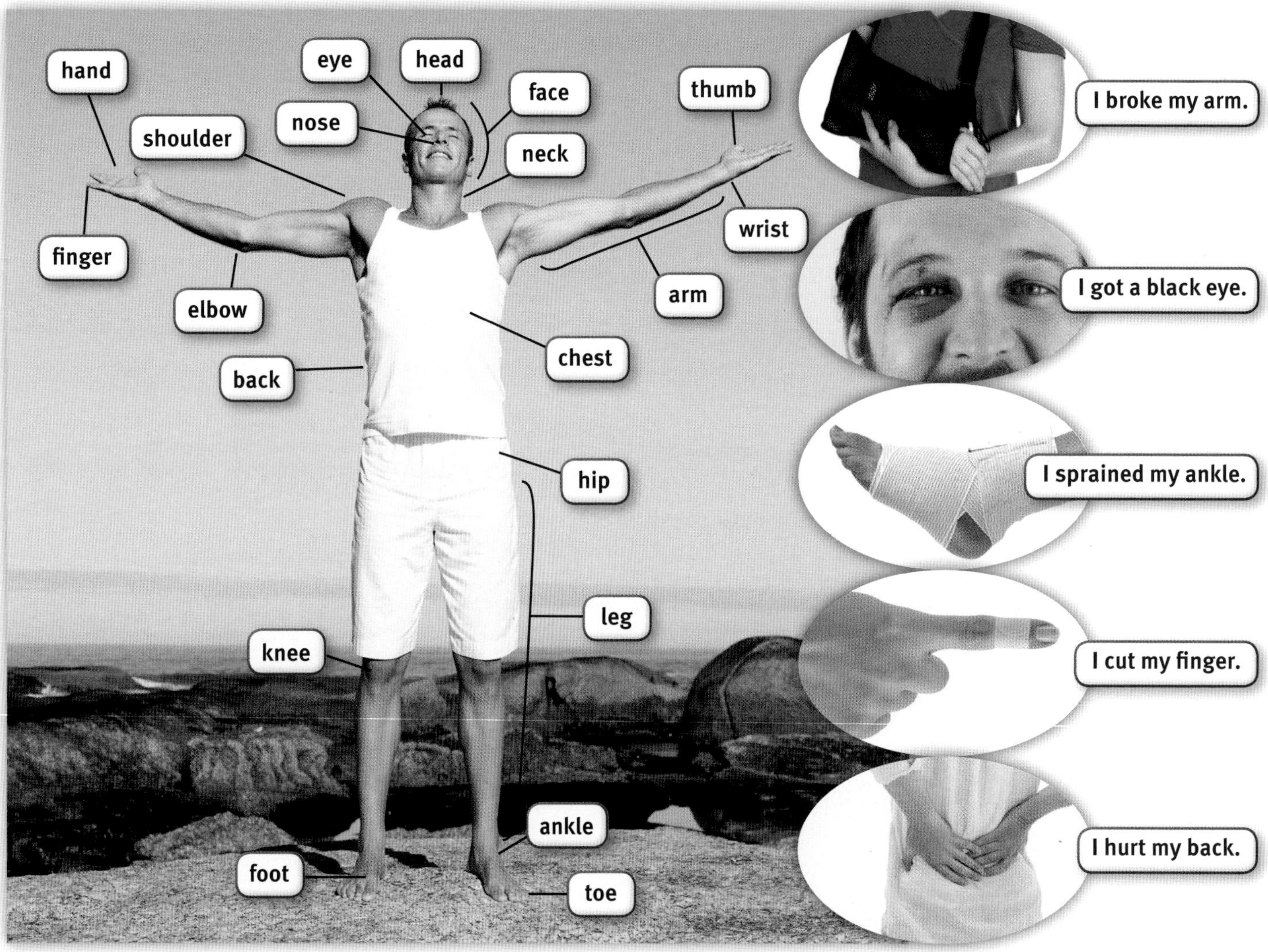

Word sort **B** Make true sentences about accidents that happened to you or people you know. Use the vocabulary above and add other words you know.

break	*I broke my leg when I was a kid.*
sprain	
cut	
hurt	
other	*My sister got a black eye . . .*

About you **C** **Pair work** Take turns telling about the accidents in your chart.

Vocabulary notebook p. 94

2 Building language

A 🔊 3.28 **Listen. What happened to George? What was he doing when it happened? Practice the conversation.**

Nikki So, how was your ski trip? Did you have a good time?
George Yeah, I guess. I sort of had an accident.
Nikki Oh, really? What happened? Did you hurt yourself?
George Yeah, I broke my leg.
Nikki Oh, no! How did it happen? I mean, what were you doing?
George Well, actually, I was talking on my cell phone. . . .
Nikki While you were skiing? That's kind of dangerous.
George Yeah, I know. But I was by myself, so I was lucky I had my cell to call for help.

Figure it out **B** **Complete the questions George's other friends asked. Use the conversation above to help you.**

1. What **were** / **did** you doing?
2. How **did it happen** / **was it happening**?
3. Did you hurt **yourself** / **you**?
4. I don't enjoy skiing **by** / **with** myself. Do you?

3 Grammar Past continuous questions; reflexive pronouns 🔊 3.29

Extra practice p. 148

Past continuous
Were you **skiing** with a friend?
No, I wasn't. I was by myself.
What **were** you **doing** (when you fell)?
I was talking on my cell phone.

Simple past
Did you **hurt** yourself?
Yes, I did.
What **did** you **do**?
I called for help.

Reflexive pronouns

I	hurt	**myself.**
You		**yourself.**
He		**himself.**
She		**herself.**
We		**ourselves.**
They		**themselves.**

In conversation
10% of uses of ***yourself*** are in the question ***How about yourself?*** Almost 10% of uses of ***myself*** are in the expression ***by myself***.

Common errors
Don't use an object pronoun when the subject and object of the verb refer to the same person.
My father hurt ***himself.***
(NOT ~~*My father hurt him*~~.)

A **Complete the conversations with reflexive pronouns and the simple past or past continuous of the verbs given.**

1. A What's wrong with your finger? Did you cut ________ ?
   B Yeah, I accidentally cut ________ with a knife.
   A Oh, ________ you ________ (make) dinner?
2. A My father hurt ________ at the gym.
   B That's too bad. ________ he ________ (lift) weights?
   A Yeah. A lot of people hurt ________ on weight machines, I guess.
3. A Hey, where ________ you ________ (get) that black eye?
   B Oh, my mom and I had a car accident. But she's OK.
   A Well, that's good. Uh, so who ________ (drive)?
4. A My sister was hiking by ________ last weekend, and she broke her ankle. She was in the middle of nowhere.
   B Oh, no! So, how ________ she ________ (get) help?
   I mean, ________ anyone else ________ (hike) on the trail?

Sounds right p. 139

B **Pair work** **Practice the conversations above. Continue them with your own ideas.**

That's hilarious.

1 Conversation strategy Reacting to a story

A Look at some words from a funny story. Can you guess what happened?

curry *phone* *burnt pan* *hide* *hilarious*

B 3.30 Listen. What happened to Hugo? How did he "solve" his problem?

Hugo I was at my friend's house one time. We were making Thai curry for a bunch of people . . .

Olivia Oh, I love Thai food.

Hugo And he left me in the kitchen to watch the curry. Well, my phone rang and I got talking . . .

Olivia Uh-oh.

Hugo . . . and it all stuck to the bottom of the pan and burned.

Olivia Oh, no!

Hugo Yeah. It didn't taste too good. I freaked.

Olivia I bet.

Hugo So I poured the curry into another pan and added some chili peppers. Then I hid the burnt pan under the sink.

Olivia Oh, that's hilarious. I bet no one even noticed.

Hugo I don't know. No one said anything, but they drank a lot of water.

C Notice how Olivia reacts to Hugo's story. She makes brief comments on the things he says to show she is listening and interested. Find examples in the conversation.

"It all stuck to the bottom of the pan and burned."
"Oh, no!"

D Read the story below and the comments on the right. For each part of the story, choose a comment. Practice telling the story and commenting with a partner.

1. I was working as a server at Pierre's last year. _c_
2. Yeah, it's very fancy with cool art and everything. _____
3. Well, it's not cheap. Anyway, I was serving coffee to this guy, and I spilled it all over his suit! _____
4. Yeah – but wait. I found out it was Pierre himself! _____
5. Yeah, and he was pretty mad. But he didn't fire me! _____

a. Oh, no! I bet he was upset.
b. Well, that was lucky.
c. Oh, Pierre's is nice, I heard.
d. Expensive, huh?
e. You're kidding, the owner?

2 Strategy plus *I bet . . .*

You can start a statement with *I bet . . .* when you are pretty sure about something.

You can also use *I bet* as a response to show you understand a situation.

A I freaked!
B I bet.

In conversation

Bet is one of the top 600 words. Over 60% of its uses are in the expression ***I bet . . .***

3.31 Read the stories and guess the responses. Then listen and write the responses you hear. Practice with a partner.

1. A A friend of mine was staying at a hotel one time, and she was walking back to her room in the dark, and she fell in the pool. Everyone at the pool café saw her!
   B Oh, no! I bet ______________________ .
2. A One time I fell asleep on the subway, and when I woke up, the train was at the end of the line. It took an hour to get back to my stop.
   B Oh, I bet ______________________ .
3. A I was on vacation in London with my parents a few years ago, and we were flying home. Anyway, we got to the airport, and I realized my passport was still in the hotel safe.
   B Oh, no. I bet ______________________ .

3 Listening and strategies A funny story

A 3.32 Listen to the story. Choose the best response each time you hear a pause. Check (✓) *a* or *b*.

1. a. ☐ That's awful. b. ☐ Oh, I bet.
2. a. ☐ I bet. b. ☐ Nice.
3. a. ☐ It's easy to do. b. ☐ That's good.
4. a. ☐ I bet. b. ☐ Thank goodness.
5. a. ☐ I bet he was pretty upset. b. ☐ Good.

About you **B 3.32 Listen to the story again. Write your own comments or responses when you hear the pauses.**

1. ______________________
2. ______________________
3. ______________________
4. ______________________
5. ______________________

C Pair work **Take turns retelling the story you just heard, or tell your own story. React with short comments and respond using *I bet*.**

1 Reading

A Brainstorm! Make a list of any good things that happened recently. Tell the class.

I passed my final math test.
My friend gave me a ticket to a concert.

B Read the article. What bad thing happened to each person? Did their stories have happy endings?

Reading tip

As you read a story, pay attention to the time expressions like *ten years later,* or *last month*. They help you follow events.

EVERY CLOUD HAS A SILVER LINING . . .

GEMMA RUSSO, CALIFORNIA

Sometimes when things go wrong, they just go wrong. But occasionally something really positive comes out of a bad situation. Last month, while I was hiking in a state park, I took a photo of an amazing sunset over a lake. It was so beautiful that I decided to text it to my friend Charley right then and there. Anyway, when I was taking more photos of the lake, I slipped and dropped my cell phone in the water. Disaster! I lost all my photos, and I sprained my ankle. They couldn't fix my phone, either. Well, apparently, Charley secretly sent in my sunset photo to the local TV station. Today, they chose it for "Photo of the Month," and I won a brand new camera! Maybe every cloud does have a silver lining, after all!

ELENA, TEXAS

Ten years ago, my scooter broke down when I was riding to school. I couldn't afford to fix it, so that semester I had to get up at 5:00 a.m. every day to take the bus. One cold, wet morning, I was feeling really tired and grumpy. But while I was waiting for the bus, this guy started talking to me, and he actually made me laugh! It turned out that he was studying at the same college. We exchanged phone numbers, and the rest is history. Ten years later, we're married with two children. Oh, and a new scooter!

CHIN-HO, DAEGU

A couple of weeks ago, I was helping a friend move his things into my apartment. He was out of work and needed a place to stay. While we were carrying some heavy boxes up the stairs, I hurt my back. It was really bad, so I had to go to the emergency room. Anyway, while I was waiting to see the doctor, I saw an advertisement for a computer technician at the hospital. I called my friend, he got the job, and I got a prescription for painkillers! At least his cloud had a silver lining! Though I do have my apartment all to myself again.

C Read the article on page 92 again. Are the sentences true or false? Check (✓) *True* (T) or *False* (F). Correct the false sentences.

	T	F
1. Gemma believes that something good ~~always~~ *occasionally* comes out of a bad situation.	☐	☑
2. Gemma won a new camera because she sent her photo to a local TV station.	☐	☐
3. Elena had to take the bus to class because she didn't have the money to fix her scooter.	☐	☐
4. Elena liked the guy at the bus stop because he was funny.	☐	☐
5. Chin-ho hurt himself when he was trying to help a friend.	☐	☐
6. Chin-ho's friend moved to a new place when he got the job at the hospital.	☐	☐

2 Listening and speaking Happy endings?

A 3.33 **Listen to Gary's and Pam's stories. Who lost something? Who got lost?**

B 3.33 **Listen to the stories again. Answer the questions.**

Gary's story

1. Where was Gary? What was he doing?
2. Who did he meet?
3. Why did he forget his briefcase?
4. What did he do when he got to work?
5. Does this story have a happy ending? Why or why not?

Pam's story

1. Where was Pam going?
2. What was her problem?
3. How did she get help?
4. How did the woman offer to help?
5. Does this story have a happy ending? Why or why not?

C Pair work Student A: Choose one of the stories above, and retell it to a partner. Student B: Listen. Did your partner leave out any important details?

Free talk pp. 134 and 136

3 Writing Anecdotes

A Think of a time something went wrong. Write 10 to 12 sentences about it. Make sure your sentences are in order.

I was walking to work last week.
It started to rain.
I didn't have an umbrella.
I put a newspaper over my head and ran.
I got to the corner.
The light changed.
I had to wait for a really long time.
A young man came up to me.
He offered to share his umbrella.
He walked with me all the way to work!

About you **B Read the Help note and the anecdote. What events do the words *when* and *while* link? Then use your notes from above to write your own anecdote.**

Last week, I was walking to work **when** it started to rain. I didn't have an umbrella, so I put a newspaper over my head and ran. **When** I got to the corner, the light changed, and I had to wait for a really long time. **While** I was waiting, a young man came up to me and offered to share his umbrella. He walked with me all the way to work! It was so nice of him.

Help note

Linking ideas with *when* and *while*.

You can use ***when*** or ***while*** to link a longer "background" event and another action.

- ***While*** emphasizes the length of time an action or event takes.
- ***When*** also shows events that happen one after another.

C Group work Read your classmates' anecdotes. Which ones show "every cloud has a silver lining"?

Learning tip *Sketches*

Draw and label pictures to help you remember new vocabulary.

In conversation

Take my hand

The top ten body parts people talk about are:

1. hand
2. eye
3. head
4. face
5. leg
6. arm
7. mouth
8. ear
9. back
10. knee

1 Label the sketch. Use the words in the box.

eye
nose
head
face
neck
shoulder

2 Now make a sketch of a body from head to toe. How many parts of the body can you label?

On your own

Before you go to sleep each night, think of the name for each part of your body. Start at your head, and work toward your toes. Can you think of each word in English before you fall asleep?

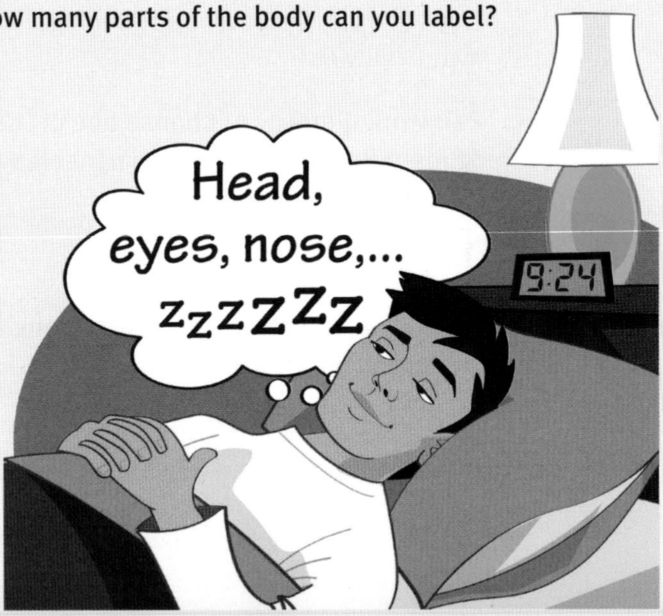

Can Do! Now I can . . .

✓ I can . . . ? I need to review how to . . .

- ☐ tell anecdotes about things that went wrong.
- ☐ talk about accidents and what happened.
- ☐ react with expressions like *Oh, no!* to show I'm listening to a story.
- ☐ use *I bet* to show I'm sure or as a response to show I understand.
- ☐ understand people telling anecdotes and respond.
- ☐ understand the details of a story.
- ☐ read anecdotes in an article.
- ☐ write an anecdote about something that went wrong.

1 Can you complete this conversation?

A Complete the conversation. Use the simple past or past continuous of the verbs.

Marty: Where *did* you *get* (get) that black eye? ________ you ________ (fall) or something?

Kevin: Not exactly. I ________ (crash) into a tree with a bike.

Marty: You're kidding! How ________ that ________ (happen)?

Kevin: Well, I ________ (ride) my little brother's bicycle. And his friends ________ (watch) me and ________ (laugh) at me.

Marty: So why ________ they ________ (laugh)? I mean, what ________ you ________ (do)?

Kevin: I ________ (not do) anything special. But the bike is kind of small.

Marty: Yeah, I bet. And I bet you ________ (try) to look cool, too.

Kevin: I guess. I ________ (look) at the kids behind me. And I ________ (not see) the tree ahead of me. When my brother ________ (shout), "Watch out," I ________ (turn) around, but it was too late.

Marty: Oh, no! ________ you ________ (hurt) yourself?

Kevin: Well, I ________ (not break) anything. I just ________ (feel) embarrassed.

B Pair work Practice the conversation. Then practice again and change Marty's responses.

2 What's in the bathroom?

A Look at the picture for ten seconds, and try to remember where things are. Then close your book. How many sentences can you write?

1. There's a toothbrush on the sink.

B Pair work Choose six items from the picture. Give your partner clues to guess the items. Then change roles.

A *You use it to clean your teeth.*
B *Is it a toothbrush?*
A *No, it's not.*
B *Is it toothpaste? . . .*

3 Can you use these expressions?

Use these words and expressions to complete the conversation. Use capital letters where necessary.

whose	yours	one	bright	would you mind	I guess	by myself	no, not at all
mine	hers	red	to do	✓ do you mind if	I bet	yourself	

Karen _Do you mind if_ I come in? You look busy.
Trish No, make __________ at home. __________ handing me that paintbrush? The red __________ ?
Karen __________ .
Trish Thanks. So, what do you think?
Karen Um, nice. I love the __________ __________ wall. Did you and your roommate choose the colors together?
Trish No, actually, I did it all __________ . Nadia's away this week.
Karen Oh, is she? __________ this was a lot of work.
Trish Actually, no. It was very easy __________ .
Karen __________ room is this? Is it __________ or Nadia's?
Trish This one is __________ , and __________ is down the hall.
Karen Um, does Nadia like these colors?
Trish I don't know. But I do! __________ I have an eye for color.

4 Suggestions, please!

Pair work Think of solutions to these problems. Then take turns making suggestions.

"I get a lot of colds in the winter."
"My bedroom is always a mess."
"I'm going camping in June, but I don't have any equipment."
"Ouch! I think I just sprained my ankle."

A ***I get a lot of colds in the winter.***
B ***Why don't you . . . ?***

5 Do you mind . . . ?

Pair work Imagine you and your partner are in a car on a road trip. One of you is the driver. Take turns asking permission and making requests. Use the ideas below and add your own.

- turn on the air conditioning
- listen to the radio
- check the GPS
- stop for a snack
- drive
- slow down
- open the window
- borrow some sunscreen
- eat one of your cookies

A ***Would you mind turning on the air conditioning?***
B ***No, not at all.***

UNIT 10

Communication

Can Do! In this unit, you learn how to . . .

Lesson A
- Compare ways of communicating using comparative adjectives

Lesson B
- Manage phone conversations
- Compare communication habits using *more*, *less*, and *fewer*

Lesson C
- Interrupt and restart a phone conversation
- Use *just* to soften what you say

Lesson D
- Read an article about texting
- Write an article giving pros and cons

Before you begin . . .

Match these ways of communicating with the pictures. Which of these do you do?

- ☐ texting
- ☐ video conferencing
- ☐ social networking
- ☐ video calling
- ☐ instant messaging (IM)

HOW DO YOU KEEP IN TOUCH WITH PEOPLE?

"Well, at work we use video conferencing for meetings with our international offices. It's less expensive than a business trip. And more convenient. And you don't get jet lag, either!"
–Kayla Johnson

"We use email at work, but I use my social network to keep in touch with friends. I was getting a lot of spam in my personal email. There's nothing worse than spam in your inbox."
–Alma Jones

"I text my friends all day. Texting's a lot quicker and easier than calling. It's more fun, too. I can't do it in class, though."
–Mayumi Sato

"Well, I video call my parents. They think it's better than the phone because they can see me. I guess it's a good way to keep in touch when I'm away at school."
–Paco Rodriguez

"Well, for birthdays and things I still like to send a card. I know regular mail is slower and less reliable than email, but cards are more personal. And I never send those e-cards. I just think it's nicer to get a real card."
–Tim Henry

1 Getting started

A 4.01 **Listen to the responses to the survey question. How do the people keep in touch?**

Figure it out **B** **Can you complete the sentences? Circle the correct words. Use the survey to help you.**

1. Mayumi says texting is **quicker** / **quick** than calling. It's more fun **than** / **that** calling, too.
2. Tim thinks real cards are more **personal** / **nice** than e-cards.
3. Kayla says that video conferencing is **less** / **more** expensive than a business trip.
4. Paco's parents think that video calling is **good** / **better** than phone calls.
5. Alma says nothing is **worse** / **bad** than spam in your inbox.

2 Grammar Comparative adjectives 4.02

Extra practice p. 149

Short adjectives *Adjective* + ***-er***	Texting is **quicker** and **easier than** calling. It's **nicer** to get a real card than an e-card.
Long adjectives ***more*** + *adjective* ***less*** + *adjective*	Real cards are **more personal than** e-cards. Video conferences are **less expensive than** trips.
Irregular adjectives ***good*** ▸ ***better*** ***bad*** ▸ ***worse***	Video calls are **better than** phone calls. Nothing is **worse than** spam in your inbox.

Notice
slow ▸ slow**er**
nice ▸ nice**r**
easy ▸ eas**ier**
big ▸ big**ger**

But
fun ▸ **more** fun

In conversation

The top adjectives after ***more*** are ***expensive***, ***convenient***, ***important***, ***interesting***, and ***fun***.

A Complete the conversations with the comparative form of the adjectives and *than* if needed. Then practice with a partner.

1. A Do you like e-cards? I think they're *more interesting than* (interesting) real cards.
   B True. And they're ____________ (easy) to send, too. Though they're a bit ____________ (personal) real cards.
2. A Do you ever use video calling? Our grandparents think it's ____________ (nice) because they can see us. It's ____________ (good) the phone.
   B Yeah, and it's ____________ (expensive) international phone calls.
3. A Do you prefer your tablet or your laptop?
   B My laptop. It's ____________ (big), but it's ____________ (useful) a tablet. Tablets are ____________ (difficult) to work on.
   A Yeah? My sister prefers her tablet. She says it's ____________ (light) her laptop, so it's ____________ (convenient) to carry around.
4. A Do you use email much these days? I don't. I just use my social network.
   B Me too. It's ____________ (efficient) email. And it's ____________ (fun). It's ____________ (good) texting, too. Texting's ____________ (bad) email.

About you **B Pair work Ask and answer the questions above. Give your own opinions.**

Common errors

With comparatives, use *more* or *-er*, not both.

*IM is **easier** than email.* (NOT *IM is ~~more easier~~ than email.*)

3 Speaking naturally Linking

With social networking, it's easier to keep in touch with people.
Text messages are less expensive than phone calls.
Real cards are nicer than e-cards.

A 4.03 Listen and repeat. Notice how the consonants are linked to the vowels.

About you **B 4.04 Listen and repeat the questions below. Then discuss the questions in groups.**

1. How do you keep in touch with friends and family?
2. Do you talk to your grandparents every day?
3. Do you use a social network to communicate with friends?
4. Is it easier to text your friends or to call them?
5. Do you think video calls are more fun than phone calls?

Lesson B On the phone

1 Building vocabulary

A 4.05 Listen and read. Why can't Nathan have a conversation with Angela?

1

Receptionist Good afternoon. Sun Company.
Nathan Hello. **Could I speak to** Angela Bell, please?
Receptionist One moment, please.
Voice mail Angela Bell is on the phone. Please leave a message.
Nathan **Hi**, Angela. **This is** Nathan. **Call me back on my cell.**

2

Angela Angela Bell.
Nathan Hi, Angela. It's Nathan. Did you get my message?
Angela Uh, yes, I think so. **Oh, hold on. I have another call**. Call me later, OK?

3

Woman Hello?
Nathan Uh, Angela?
Woman No, this is Beth.
Nathan Oh, **I'm sorry. I think I have the wrong number.**
Woman No problem.

4

Angela Hello?
Nathan Hi, Angela. Guess what!
Angela Nathan, I can't hear you. **You're breaking up**. Call me back on my office phone.
Nathan Oh, OK.

5

Angela Angela Bell.
Nathan Angela! Listen. My boss has some concert tickets for us. . . . Uh, Angela? Angela? Oh, no! **We got cut off.**

Word sort **B Find these expressions in the phone conversations, and write them in the chart. Then practice the conversations with a partner.**

What can you say when . . .	
you ask to speak to someone?	
you leave a voice-mail message?	
you want someone to return your call?	
you need to interrupt because you have another call?	
you call someone by mistake?	
you can't hear some of the other person's words?	
the phone call suddenly ends?	

2 Building language

A 4.06 **Listen to the conversation Nathan and Angela finally have. Why was Nathan calling?**

Nathan Finally! It's hard to get ahold of you.
Angela You're not that easy to reach, either.
Nathan You spend a lot more time on the phone than I do.
Angela That's because I get more calls.
Nathan You just talk more! Anyway, I was calling before 'cause my boss had free tickets to the Sting concert tonight.
Angela Oh, great! What time?
Nathan Well, it's too late now. He gave them to someone else.
Angela Oh, no! Why didn't you send me a text message?

Figure it out **B Can you rewrite these sentences and keep the same meaning? Start with the word given. Use the conversation above to help you.**

1. Angela You get fewer calls than I do. I ______________________.
2. Nathan I spend less time on the phone than you do. You ______________________.
3. Nathan I talk less than you do. You ______________________.

3 Grammar *More, less, fewer* 4.07

Extra practice p. 149

With countable nouns	With uncountable nouns	With verbs
I get **more** calls than you (do).	I spend **more** time on the phone.	She talks **more** than he does.
You get **fewer** calls than I do.	You spend **less** time on the phone.	He talks **less** than she does.

In conversation

Fewer is not very common. People use it more in writing.

About you **A Complete the sentences with *more*, *less*, or *fewer* so they are true for you. Rewrite them in a different way and keep the same meaning.**

1. My friends talk *more* than I do. *I talk less than my friends do.*
2. On the phone, I listen ________ than I talk.
3. I send ________ emails than texts.
4. I spend ________ time on social networking sites than my parents.
5. I get ________ emails than I did two years ago.
6. I get ________ voice-mail messages than text messages.
7. My parents talk on the phone a lot ________ than I do.
8. I like texting ________ than calling.

B Pair work **Discuss the sentences above. Compare your styles of communication.**

A *I think my friends talk more than I do. I'm pretty quiet.*
B *Really? I talk more than all my friends. They say I never stop talking!*

Sounds right p. 139

What were you saying?

1 Conversation strategy Dealing with interruptions

A What kinds of things can interrupt phone conversations? Make a list.

B 4.08 Listen. What does Maria want to tell Sarah?

Sarah Hello?

Maria Hi, Sarah. It's Maria.

Sarah Hey. How are you doing?

Maria Great. Listen, I have some news. Juan and I went out to a fancy restaurant last night and . . .

Sarah Oh, just a minute. I've got another call. Hold on a second. . . . Sorry. So, what were you saying?

Maria Well, guess what? We're getting married.

Sarah That's wonderful! Congratulations!

Maria Thanks. So yeah, the wedding's going to be in . . .

Sarah Oh, sorry. Now there's someone's at the door. Hold on. . . . OK. So, you were saying?

Maria Well, I was just calling to ask – will you be my maid of honor?

Sarah Are you kidding? Of course!

C Notice how Sarah interrupts the conversation and then comes back to it with expressions like these. Find examples in the conversation.

Interrupting a conversation:	Restarting the conversation:
Just a minute / second.	*What were you saying?*
Excuse me just a second.	*You were saying?*
I'm sorry. Hold on (a second).	*Where were we?*
Could / Can you hold on a second?	*What were we talking about?*

D 4.09 Listen. Complete these phone conversations with the expressions you hear. Then practice with a partner. Continue the conversations using your own ideas.

1. A So yeah. I just read on a friend's social networking page that . . .
   B Oh, ________________ . . . . I need my charger. OK. Got it. So, ________________ ?

2. A Anyway, my teacher told me . . .
   B Oh, ________________ . My toast is burning. Let me just – gosh . . . OK. ________________ .
   So, yeah. ________________ ?

3. A Sorry about that. I dropped my phone. So, ________________ ?
   B You said your social life is more important than your job. Oh, ________________ .
   Um, a coffee, please. Sorry. I'm at a coffee shop. So, ________________ ?

2 Strategy plus *just*

You can use the word *just* to make the things you say softer.

4.10 Listen to four phone conversations. Write *just* each time the speakers use it. Then practice the conversations with a partner.

In conversation
Just is one of the top 30 words.

1. A Hi there. Do you have a minute? I just want to tell you some good news.
   B Really? Hold on a second. I need to close the door.

2. A Hello?
   B Hi, Dad. It's me. Is Mom there?
   A Yeah. But hold on a second. She's upstairs. I need to call her.

3. A Is this a good time to talk?
   B Sure. Could you hold on a second? Let me turn down the TV. . . . So, what's up?
   A Well, I was calling to ask your advice about something.

4. A Hi, I'm calling to say hello.
   B Oh, hi. Listen, can I call you back? I have to finish something.

3 Listening and strategies Sorry about that!

A 4.11 Listen to the conversations. Why is each person calling? Write the reasons under the pictures.

1 

____

2 

____

3 

____

B 4.11 Listen again. Check (✓) the reasons for the two interruptions in each conversation.

1. ☐ She got another call.
   ☐ They lost the connection.
   ☐ Her battery ran out.
   ☐ She ordered a coffee.

2. ☐ The TV wasn't working.
   ☐ There was traffic noise.
   ☐ She dropped her phone.
   ☐ The pizza arrived.

3. ☐ He had to find his wallet.
   ☐ He met a friend.
   ☐ He went the store.
   ☐ She had to turn off the oven.

About you **C Pair work** **Student A: "Call" and tell your partner some interesting news. Student B: "Answer" your partner's call. Interrupt and restart the conversation twice. Then change roles.**

A Hey, Jake. How are you? Do you have a minute? I just want to tell you something.
B Hi. So, what's going on? Oh, hold on a second. I need to take this call. It's my mom.

Vocabulary notebook p. 106

Lesson D Texting

1 Reading

A Is texting a good way to communicate? Why or why not? Make a list of reasons.

B Read the article. What's one advantage of texting? What's one disadvantage?

Reading tip

Read the first and last paragraph of an article to get a general sense of what it is about.

15 Comments

Why all the interest in texting?

ICYC*: Textese Today
(*In Case You're Curious)

LOL – Laugh out loud

:-) – Smile

SUP – What's up?

FBM – Fine by me

OTOH – On the other hand

IMO – In my opinion

An article on the Internet recently caught my eye. It was about the Texting Championships in New York City. The 17-year-old winner texted 149 characters in 39 seconds and won $50,000. That is certainly impressive, and much, much faster than me – LOL :-). However, I started to wonder: Why is there still so much interest in texting? After all, texting is a commonplace activity these days.

It's clear that texting, with all its abbreviations and symbols, is now part of our lives. According to research, about 75% of Americans send text messages, and almost one third prefer to text rather than talk on their phone. It's just quicker to send a text than make a call. Typing SUP is faster than asking "How are you?" and listening to the answer. It's also more discreet because no one can overhear your conversation – and that's FBM.

OTOH, texting has its downsides, too, and perhaps it's these problems that create all the interest. Texters gripe that they are getting more spam texts than ever before. Teachers complain that students' test scores are getting worse because teens spend more time texting than they should. Some also say that texting encourages bad grammar and punctuation and IMO, that's true. Students don't realize they shouldn't write their essays in "textese," and they get low grades as a result. Many young people are sleeping less because they wake up in the night every time a text pops up on their phone. Others have injuries to their hands and thumbs from the constant texting.

There are also more serious problems with texting, however, such as the accidents that happen when people text and drive at the same time. Fortunately, many countries are passing laws that make it illegal to text when you're behind the wheel of a car. In addition, public service advertisements warn of the dangers of texting while driving. Perhaps, then, there is good reason for all the interest in texting.

C **Read the article again and answer the questions. Then compare with a partner.**

1. Why do so many people like texting better than talking on the phone? Find two reasons.
2. How many texting abbreviations does the author of the article use? What does each one mean?
3. What is "textese"? What kinds of problems does it cause?
4. What are some other downsides of texting? Find four problems in the article.
5. Do you have any advice for people who text all the time? Write four "Dos" and "Don'ts" for texters.

D **Find the expressions below in the article on page 104. What do they mean? Match each one to a definition. Write *a* to *f*.**

1. caught my eye ____
2. wonder ____
3. discreet ____
4. overhear ____
5. downsides ____
6. warn of ____

a. disadvantages
b. not noticeable
c. hear without intending to
d. got my attention
e. say there's a problem
f. ask myself

2 Speaking and listening It can be annoying . . .

About you **A** **Pair work Read the sentences below. Which ones do you agree with? What else can you say about texting?**

- ☐ Texting takes less time than calling.
- ☐ Texting your parents in public is less embarrassing than talking on the phone.
- ☐ Texting is useful when you ask a favor.
- ☐ It's annoying to get texts late at night.
- ☐ When you're with a friend, it's OK to text other friends.
- ☐ You shouldn't text friends during class.

B 4.12 **Listen to Vanessa talk about texting. Check (✓) the sentences she agrees with.**

3 Writing The pros and cons

A **Pair work Choose one of these ways of communicating. Make a list of its advantages and disadvantages.**

- video calling
- texting
- social networking
- phone calls
- email

Advantages of video calling
- *It's fun to video call with a close friend.*
- *It's either very cheap or free.*
- *It's almost like you're in the same room.*

Disadvantages of video calling
- *People call me when I don't look very good. It's embarrassing!*
- *People talk longer on a video call. It's harder to say good-bye.*

B **The article below is divided into four sections. What is the purpose of each section? Read the Help note for an explanation. Then use your list from above to write a similar article.**

Home | Edit | Document Elements | Tables | Table Layout | Charts | Smart Art

The Pros and Cons of Video Calling

Video calling is becoming more and more popular, and some of my friends now call me every day.

It's fun to video call with a close friend if you don't see him or her very often. It's almost like you're in the same room.

On the other hand, video calls can be a problem. Sometimes you don't want people to see you, and it can be embarrassing! Also, people talk longer on a video call than a phone call. For some reason, it's harder to say good-bye!

In my opinion, video calling is good for friends you don't see very often. However, for friends from class, a quick text message or call is much better.

Help note

Writing an article giving pros and cons
- Write an introduction to the topic.
- Write about the advantages.
- Write about the disadvantages.
  However, . . .
  On the other hand, . . .
- Write a conclusion, giving your views.
  I think . . .
  In my opinion, . . .

Free talk p. 134

About you **C** **Group work Read your classmates' articles. Whose opinions do you agree with?**

Learning tip *Learning expressions*

One way to learn expressions is to make a note of the situations when you can use them.

In conversation

Hold on!

People mostly say ***Hold on*** to leave a phone conversation for a minute.

Hold on.

Hang on.

Just a minute.

1 Match the expressions with the situations.

1. "I'm sorry. I have the wrong number."____
2. "I have another call." ____
3. "You're breaking up."____
4. "We got cut off." ____
5. "Where were we?" ____

a. You can't hear someone clearly.
b. You call the wrong number by mistake.
c. You come back to a conversation after an interruption.
d. You get a signal that a second person is calling you.
e. You suddenly can't hear the other person at all.

2 Make a chart of expressions you can use on the phone when . . .

- you have problems getting ahold of someone
- you have problems with the call while you're talking.
- you ask if it's a good time to talk.
- you need to interrupt the conversation.
- you ask to speak to someone.
- you explain why you're calling.
- you restart the conversation.
- you can't talk now, but you can talk later.

On your own

Make a phrase book for different situations – for example, making calls. Carry it with you, and learn the phrases.

Can Do! Now I can . . .

✓ I can. . .   ? I need to review how to . . .

- ☐ talk about different ways of communicating.
- ☐ make comparisons.
- ☐ manage phone conversations.
- ☐ interrupt and restart phone conversations.
- ☐ use *just* to soften what I say.
- ☐ understand basic phone conversations.
- ☐ understand someone giving opinions about texting.
- ☐ read an article about the pros and cons of texting.
- ☐ write an article giving pros and cons.

Appearances

UNIT 11

Can Do! In this unit, you learn how to . . .

Lesson A
- Describe people's appearance using adjectives and *have* and *have got*

Lesson B
- Identify people by their appearance, actions, or location using verb + *-ing* and prepositions

Lesson C
- Use expressions like *What do you call . . . ?* if you can't remember a word
- Use expressions like *You mean . . . ?* to check or suggest words and names

Lesson D
- Read an article about fashion
- Write an article about fashion trends

Before you begin . . .

Look at the picture. Can you find someone who . . .

- is short?
- is tall?
- is young?
- is old?
- is thin?
- is heavy?
- has long hair?
- has short hair?
- has dark hair?
- has blond hair?

Lesson A Family traits

*six (foot) three = one meter ninety

1 Getting started

A **Describe the people in the picture above. Can you find someone with curly hair? With straight hair? Someone who is tall and skinny?**

B 🔊 4.13 **Listen. Alice and Heather are meeting Heather's twin sister, Hayley, at the airport. Can you find Hayley in the picture? Practice the conversation.**

Figure it out **C** **Use the conversation above to help you complete these questions and answers. Then practice with a partner.**

1. A ________ does your sister look like?
   B She's tall, and she's ________ blond hair.

2. A ________ tall is your sister?
   B Six foot three. We're different. We don't look ________ .

2 Grammar Describing people; *have got* 4.14

Extra practice p. 150

Do Hayley and Heather **look alike**?
No, they look totally different.

What does Hayley **look like**?
She's tall and thin.

Who does she **look like**?
She looks like her father.

How tall is her father?
He's six (foot) seven.
He's over two meters tall.

What color is Hayley's hair?
It's blond.

What color are Hayley's eyes?
They're blue.

Saying heights
Her father is six (foot) seven. He's six foot seven inches (tall).
She's one meter ninety (tall).

have got = have
Does she **have** curly hair?
No, she**'s got** straight hair.
Who**'s got** curly hair?
I do. I**'ve got** curly hair.

Who's got = Who has got
I've got = I have got
He's got = He has got

Common errors

Don't confuse these questions:
What's she like?
= What kind of person is she?
What does she look like?
= Can you describe her?

A **Choose the correct words to complete the questions. Compare with a partner.**

1. (**How**) / **What** tall are you?
2. What color **have** / **are** your eyes?
3. **Who** / **What** do you look like – your mother or your father?
4. **What** / **How** color is your mother's hair? **Is it** / **Are they** long or short?
5. **What** / **How** does your father look like?
6. Does anyone in your family **have** / **got** blue eyes?
7. Who **'s got** / **got** short hair in your class? Does anyone **got** / **have** long hair?
8. Do any of your friends look **alike** / **like** someone famous?
9. Do you know any twins? Do they look exactly **like** / **alike**?

Common errors

Don't forget to use a form of *have*.

*She's **got** long brown hair.*
(NOT ~~*She got*~~ *long brown hair.*)

About you **B** **Pair work** **Ask and answer the questions above. Give your own information.**

3 Speaking naturally Checking information

Asking for information	*A What's his **name**?*	*A How **old** is he?*	*A What color is his **hair**?*
	B Joshua Murray.	*B Ninety-five.*	*B White.*
Checking information	*A **What's** his name?*	*A **How** old is he?*	*A **What** color is his hair?*

A 4.15 **Listen and repeat the questions and answers above. Notice how the stress and intonation are different in the checking questions.**

About you **B** **Pair work** **Ask your partner to describe a good friend. Ask information questions and checking questions to make sure your information is correct.**

A ***So, tell me about your friend. What's her name?***
B ***Her name's Kat.***
A ***What's her name?***
B ***Kat. It's short for Katrina.***

1 Building vocabulary

A 4.16 Listen and say the sentences. Check (✓) the features you like. Tell the class.

"I like mustaches." *"I like muscular people."*

1

☐ He has **a beard** and **a mustache**.

2

☐ She has **pierced ears**.

3

☐ He has **a shaved head**. He's **bald**.

4

☐ She wears **braces**.

5

☐ She has **long fingernails**.

6

☐ He wears his hair in **a ponytail**.

7

☐ She's got **freckles**.

8

☐ She wears her hair in **cornrows**.

9

☐ She wears **glasses**.

10

☐ He's very **muscular**.

11

☐ She wears **braids**.

12

☐ He's got **spiked hair**.

Word sort **B** For each feature, think of someone you know, and write a sentence. Then compare with a partner.

1. My boss has a beard and a mustache.
2. My mother's got pierced ears.

Vocabulary notebook p. 116

2 Building language

A 4.17 **Listen. Find Rosa's roommate and Rosa's brother in the picture. Practice the conversation.**

Jason So, is your new roommate here?
Rosa Ava? Yeah, she's right over there.
Jason Oh, which one is she?
Rosa She's the woman standing by the table.
Jason The one with the short hair?
Rosa No, the woman with the ponytail.
Jason Oh, she looks nice. And who's that guy talking to her? He looks kind of weird.
Rosa You mean the guy in the yellow pants? That's my brother Jimmy.

Figure it out **B Can you complete these sentences about Ava and Jimmy? Use the conversation above to help you.**

1. Ava is the woman ________ by the table.
   She's the one ________ the ponytail.
2. Jimmy is the guy ________ to Ava.
   He's the one ________ the yellow pants.

3 Grammar Phrases with verb + *-ing* and prepositions 4.18

Extra practice p. 150

Which one is your roommate?
She's the woman **standing** by the table. / **wearing** (the) black pants.
She's the one **by** the table. / **with** (the) long hair. / **in** the black shirt.

Who's the guy **talking** to Rosa's roommate?
The guy **wearing** (the) yellow pants? My brother.
The guy **standing** by the table is my brother.

Who's the guy **in** the blue shirt?
Which one? The one **with** (the) glasses? That's Jason.
The guy **with** / **in** (the) yellow pants is Rosa's brother.

A Choose the correct words in the questions. Then look at the picture above, and match the questions and answers. Ask and answer the questions with a partner.

1. Who's the tall man **in** / **in the** striped shirt? _c_
2. Who's the woman **talks** / **talking** to Jimmy? ____
3. Who's the guy **with** / **in** the shaved head? ____
4. Who's the woman **stand** / **standing** by Alex? ____
5. Who's the woman **in** / **with** the black curly hair? ____
6. Is Jason the one **is eating** / **eating** a cookie? ____

a. Yes. He's the one talking to Rosa.
b. In the white skirt and red top? That's Olivia.
c. In the yellow pants? That's Jimmy.
d. The muscular one? That's Alex.
e. The short blond one? That's Ava.
f. The one in the green blouse? That's Rosa.

About you **B Pair work** **Ask and answer questions about people in your class.**

A Who's the guy sitting next to Claudia?
B The one in the blue shirt? That's Marco.

Sounds right p. 139

Lesson C Conversation strategies What's his name?

1 Conversation strategy Trying to remember words

A Do you know what these things are? Match the words and the descriptions.

1. a goatee _____
2. a wig _____
3. cargo pants _____
4. platform shoes _____

a. shoes with thick soles
b. baggy pants with pockets
c. a little short beard
d. false hair

B 4.19 Listen. What does Gabby tell Jin-ho about their old classmate?

Gabby Do you remember that cool guy in our class last year? Oh, what's his name? You know . . . he always wore those baggy pants with all the pockets. What do you call them?

Jin-ho You mean cargo pants.

Gabby Yeah. And he had long hair and a funny little beard . . . what do you call that?

Jin-ho Do you mean a goatee? . . . Oh, I know. You mean Max!

Gabby That's right, Max. Well, don't look now, but he's sitting right behind you. And he's wearing a suit and tie and everything.

Jin-ho A suit and tie? No way!

Gabby Yeah, and he's got short hair. He looks different!

C Notice how Gabby uses expressions like these when she can't remember a name or a word. Find examples in the conversation.

What's his / her name?
What do you call it / them?
What do you call that . . . / those . . . ?

D Complete the conversations with expressions like the ones above. Then practice with a partner.

1. A Do you remember when everyone wore those shoes – ____________ – the ones with really thick soles?
   B Oh, yeah. Platform shoes. Actually, people still wear them!

2. A A friend of mine wears her hair in those tiny braids – ____________?
   B Cornrows? They're really cool.

3. A Who's that singer with all the amazing clothes? ____________? You know, her hair always looks different because she wears those, uh – ____________?
   B Do you mean wigs? Are you thinking of Lady Gaga?

2 Strategy plus *You mean . . .*

You can say *You mean . . .* or ask *Do you mean . . . ?* to check what someone is talking about or to suggest a word or name.

What words are these people trying to think of? Write a response using *You mean . . .* or *Do you mean . . . ?* Then practice with a partner.

1. A I'm going to buy a pair of those baggy pants with lots of pockets. What do you call them?
   B *You mean cargo pants.*
2. A My brother has long hair, and he pulls it back, you know, he wears it in a, um . . .
   B ____________
3. A My best friends are twins. They look exactly alike. They're, uh, what do you call them?
   B ____________
4. A My friend has these cute little spots on her nose. What do you call them?
   B ____________
5. A My grandfather doesn't have any hair. He's, uh, what do you call that?
   B ____________
6. A When I was a kid, I wore those, what do you call those things on your teeth. Um, . . .
   B ____________

3 Listening and strategies Celebrities

A 4.20 **Listen. Two friends are watching an awards ceremony on TV, and they are talking about the celebrities. Who are they talking about? Number the pictures 1 to 6.**

☐ Angelina Jolie ☐ Zhang Ziyi ☐ Salma Hayek ☐ Scarlett Johansson ☐ Lucy Liu ☐ Penélope Cruz

B Pair work **Take turns talking about celebrities as if you can't remember their names. Can your partner guess who you are talking about?**

A I really like that singer from Colombia. What's her name? She sings in English, Spanish, and Arabic.
B Oh, do you mean Shakira? Yeah, her voice is amazing.

Free talk pp. 135 and 136

Lesson D Changing fashions

1 Reading

A **What clothes and hairstyles are in fashion right now? When did they become fashionable?**

B **Read the blog. Which styles do you know about? Which do you like?**

Reading tip

Practice skimming. Read the first sentence of each paragraph to get a general idea of what the article is about.

http://www.fashionstatement...

BLOG FASHION TRENDS PICTURES RUNWAY SHOWS SALES CONTRIBUTE

FASHION STATEMENTS

A few days ago, I pointed out my twelve-year-old niece to a friend. "She's the one wearing braces – the *pink* ones." I realized at that moment that *braces* are now a fashion statement. Can you imagine? But then, did you ever imagine that plastic shoes with holes in them would become so popular all those years ago? Or that you could buy little charms to wear on them?

But that's the great thing about fashion. You're never quite sure what's going to become the "in" thing.

Take glasses. Big glasses came and went, and then everyone wanted designer glasses with a logo. Men wore glasses with heavy, black frames for a time. Then colored frames were the "in" thing, and soon people didn't want frames at all. Glasses, too, became a fashion statement, and people wore them even if they didn't *need* glasses!

Hairstyles are another great way to make a fashion statement. Men with ponytails, shaved heads, cornrows – they've all come and gone and come back into style again. Women's hairstyles are long and straight one minute, and short and curly the next. Bangs are in. Oh wait, no . . . bangs are out.

Then of course, there are jeans. Straight-legged are the way to go, until everyone wears them flared. Some guys wear them baggy. *Really* baggy. Women, on the other hand, seem to prefer "skinny jeans." Black jeans are in, and then everyone starts wearing white jeans, or pink jeans, or . . . every other color.

One thing is for sure. It's a lot of work keeping up with the latest fashion trends – and *expensive*! Maybe the best way to make a fashion statement is to do your own thing and not follow fashions at all!

C Read the blog again. Answer the questions.

1. Why does the writer say that braces are now a "fashion statement"?
2. What shoe style became popular years ago?
3. What five styles of glasses does the writer mention? Do you know anyone who wears any of them?
4. How many hairstyles for men does the writer list? Do you have any friends with these styles?
5. What is the opposite of baggy jeans? straight-legged jeans? Which style do you prefer?
6. What advice does the writer give about keeping up with the latest fashion trends? Do you agree?

2 Listening What's in style?

A 4.21 Listen to a fashion editor interview four people. What items are they talking about? Write the number of the conversations (1 to 4) next to the items. There is one extra item.

shirts ____ shoes ____ skirts ____ dresses ____ pants ____

B 4.21 Listen again. What specific fashion is each person talking about? How does the person feel about that style? Complete the chart. Do you agree with each person?

	Fashion	Does she / he like it? Why or why not?
1. Leslie		
2. Emery		
3. Kara		
4. Franz		

3 Speaking and writing Fashion trends

About you

A Group work Ask and answer the questions. Take notes on the different ideas.

1. What clothes are "in" today among your friends?
2. What clothes are going out of style?
3. What styles of shoes are your friends wearing?
4. What do you like about today's "look"?
5. What don't you like about it?

B Read the article below and the Help note. Underline the expressions in the article that describe trends.

Home Edit Document Elements Tables Table Layout Charts Smart Art

Casual Clothes Are Now the Rule!

This year, all my co-workers are wearing casual clothes to work. Men are wearing casual slacks and sweaters, and suits and ties are out of style. Leather shoes are "out," and dressy sneakers are "in."

It's also fashionable for women to wear slacks, and fewer women are wearing suits. High heels are going out of style. In general, I like this fashion trend. I feel more comfortable.

Help note

Describing new trends

Short hair is ***in style****.*
Long hair is going ***out of style****.*
High heels are ***dated / old-fashioned****.*
Glasses are becoming ***popular****.*
It's fashionable *to wear . . .*

Less formal expressions

Short hair is ***"in"*** *or* ***"out."***
Glasses are the ***"in" thing****.*
They're very ***trendy****.*

C Write an article describing the current "look." Use at least four of the expressions in the Help note.

Learning tip *Writing true sentences*

Use your new vocabulary in true sentences about yourself or people you know.

1 What do these people look like? Match the sentences and people.

1. He's tall, and he's got spiked hair. _d_
2. She has short hair. ____
3. He's bald, and he wears glasses. ____
4. She's wearing earrings. ____
5. She wears her hair in braids. ____
6. He's short and a little heavy. ____
7. She's got freckles. ____
8. She has long hair and big brown eyes. ____
9. He's got blue eyes and blond hair. ____
10. She has dark curly hair. ____

a

b

c

d

e

2 Write three sentences about each of these people. What do they look like?

- a family member
- a classmate
- a close friend
- yourself
- another person

On your own

Look at three different people this week.
Think of how to describe them.
Then write sentences.

Can Do! Now I can . . .

✓ I can . . . ? I need to review how to . . .

- ☐ describe people's appearance and features.
- ☐ identify people by saying what they are doing, how they look, or where they are.
- ☐ use expressions like *What do you call . . . ?* when I'm trying to remember a word.
- ☐ use *(Do) you mean. . . ?* to check or suggest a word.
- ☐ understand which person someone is describing.
- ☐ understand people's opinions about fashion.
- ☐ read an article about fashion trends.
- ☐ write an article about fashion trends.

Looking ahead

UNIT 12

Can Do! In this unit, you learn how to . . .

Lesson A
- Make predictions and discuss future plans with *will*, *may*, and *might*

Lesson B
- Talk about jobs
- Discuss future plans using the simple present in *if* and time clauses

Lesson C
- Make offers and promises with *will*
- Agree to something using *All right* and *OK*

Lesson D
- Read an article about the future
- Write an article about an invention using *first*, *second*, etc. to list ideas

Before you begin . . .

Which of these things do you think you are going to do in the next five years? How sure are you? Absolutely sure? Pretty sure? Not at all sure?

- get an interesting job
- find your own place
- move to a new city
- travel to another country

WHAT ARE YOUR PLANS FOR NEXT YEAR?

1 "Well, I'm graduating from college next June, so I guess I'll look for a job. I know it won't be easy to find one – so I may go on for a master's degree. We'll see."
–Christy Lewis

2 "I'm not sure. I might look for a better job. Before that, though, I'm going to ask my boss for a promotion. But I probably won't get one, so . . ."
–Laura Chang

3 "Well, some of my friends are going to travel around Europe for two months. I hope I'll be able to go with them. But it'll be expensive, and I might not be able to afford it."
–Paul Reade

4 "We're going to have a baby in March, so both of us will probably take some time off from work. I'm sure the baby will keep us both very busy."
–Jim and Katie Conley

5 "I'm going to retire – I'll be 65 in June – and my wife's already retired. So we'll probably move to Florida in the fall, or maybe Arizona. We're not going to spend another winter here – that's for sure!"
–Joe Etta

1 Getting started

A 4.22 **Are you going to do any of these things next year? Tell the class. Then listen. What are the people above going to do? Check (✓) the boxes below.**

☐ have a baby
☐ ask for a promotion
☐ graduate from college
☐ go on for a master's degree
☐ buy a house
☐ go on a trip
☐ retire
☐ get married

Figure it out **B Complete the sentences using the interviews above to help you.**

1. Paul says it ________ be expensive to go to Europe. He's sure about that.
2. Laura thinks she probably ________ get a promotion. She's 95% certain her boss will say no.
3. Christy says she ________ study for a master's degree. She's not sure, though.
4. Laura says she ________ look for a better job. She says it's possible.
5. Joe says he ________ retire next June. He's already decided.

2 Grammar Future with *will*, *may*, and *might* 4.23

Extra practice p. 151

You can use *will* to give facts or predictions about the future.

I'**ll** be 65 in June.
It'**ll** be expensive to travel around Europe.
The baby **will** keep us busy!
It **won't** be easy to find a job.

I'll = I will *won't = will not*

To show you are not 100% sure about the future, you can use *may* and *might*.

I **may** go on for a master's degree.
I **might not** be able to afford it.

You can also use *will* with expressions like *I guess*, *I think*, *maybe*, and *probably*.

We'**ll probably** take some time off from work.
Maybe we'**ll** move to Arizona.

Avoid *will* to talk about plans or decisions already made. Use the present continuous or *be going to*.

I'**m going** to Europe next year. I'**m going to visit** Paris. (NOT ~~I will go to Europe next year. I will visit Paris~~.)

Common errors

Don't use *can* for predictions. Use *may* or *might*.

*I **may** go away for vacation.*
(NOT *I ~~can~~ go away for vacation.*)

A Circle the correct options in the conversations below. Compare and practice in groups of three.

1. A What are you going to do at the end of this course?
   B I'm not sure. I guess **I take** / **(I'll take)** another course.
   C I don't know. **I'm going to** / **I may** travel abroad with my brother. He thinks his classes **might** / **can** finish early this year, so we **might** / **will be able to** go in May.

2. A Are your friends going away for vacation next summer?
   B Well, they **'re all going to do** / **will all do** different things. One friend **is going** / **will go** to Istanbul. I'd love to go, too, but I don't know. **I won't** / **I might not** be able to afford it.
   C Four of my friends **will** / **may** be 21, so we **'re having** / **have** a big party. It's going to be fun.

3. A Are you going to look for a new job next year?
   B Actually, I just got a new job. **I'll** / **I'm going to** work for the local newspaper. How about you?
   C I don't know. I think **I'm studying** / **I'll study** for a certificate in nutrition. I mean, **I'll** / **I may** probably go back to school because I'm pretty sure **I won't** / **I might not** get a job.

About you **B Group work** **Ask and answer the questions. Give your own answers. Who has interesting plans?**

3 Speaking naturally Reduction of *will*

Do you think . . .	*your best friend **will** always be your friend?*	*(friend'**ll**)*
	*the teacher **will** be a millionaire someday?*	*(teacher'**ll**)*
	*your parents **will** ever move to another city?*	*(parents'**ll**)*
	*all your friends **will** have children?*	*(friends'**ll**)*
	*anyone in the class **will** be famous someday?*	*(class'**ll**)*

A 4.24 **Listen and repeat the questions above. Practice the reduction of *will* to *'ll*.**

About you **B Pair work** **Ask and answer the questions. Think of more questions to ask about the future.**

A ***Do you think your best friend will always be your friend?***
B ***Well, we might not always live near each other, but I think we'll always be friends.***

1 Building vocabulary

A 4.25 **Listen and say the words. Then make a class list of other jobs and professions. Do you know anyone with these jobs?**

"My neighbor is a firefighter. She loves her job."

"My cousin may become a veterinarian at an animal hospital."

Note
You can also say:
She works ***for*** *a (computer) company.*
He works ***at*** *a hospital / grocery store.*

Word sort **B** **Complete the chart with jobs from above. Add your own ideas. Then compare with a partner.**

Who . . .

has an interesting job?	has a rewarding job?	has a difficult job?	earns a lot of money?
journalists *interior designers*	*nurses*		

"I think journalists have an interesting job. They travel a lot, and . . ."

Vocabulary notebook p. 126

2 Building language

A 🔊 4.26 Listen. What is Becca's problem? Practice the conversation.

Drew I can't believe we just have one more year of college!
Becca I know.
Drew What are you going to do when you graduate?
Becca Well, I may go to law school if I get good grades next year.
Drew Oh, I'm sure you will.
Becca Well, you never know. My parents will be disappointed if I don't go into law. They're both lawyers.
Drew Wow. That's a lot of pressure.
Becca Yeah. And after I graduate, I'll be able to work in their firm.
Drew Uh-huh. Well, that's good.
Becca Yeah, but I don't really want to be a lawyer. . . . I want to be a journalist. I guess I need to decide before I go home for the summer.
Drew Well, good luck!

Figure it out **B Choose the correct words to complete these sentences about Becca.**

1. Becca may go to law school when she **graduates** / **will graduate** from college.
2. If Becca **doesn't** / **won't** go into law, her parents will be disappointed.
3. She needs to decide before she **will go** / **goes** home for the summer.

3 Grammar Present tense verbs with future meaning 🔊 4.27

Extra practice p. 151

In complex sentences about the future, use the simple present after *if*, *when*, *after*, and *before*.

What are you going to do **when** you **graduate**?
If I **get** good grades, I may go to law school.
My parents will be disappointed **if** I **don't go** into law.
After I **graduate**, I'll be able to work in their firm.
I need to decide **before** I **go** home for the summer.

About you **A Choose the correct verbs. Then complete the sentences with your own ideas.**

1. Before this semester **will be** / **(is)** over, I think I'll be able to ______________ .
2. I'll probably ______________ after I **finish** / **will finish** my studies.
3. If I **don't** / **won't** get a good job after I **will graduate** / **graduate**, I might ______________ .
4. If I **earn** / **will earn** a lot of money in the next ten years, I may ______________ .
5. I'd like to ______________ when I **visit** / **will visit** my relatives again.
6. If I **become** / **will become** really fluent in English, I hope I'll be able to ______________ .
7. I think I'll ______________ after I **retire** / **will retire**.

B Pair work **Compare your sentences. Ask your partner questions for more information.**

A *Before this semester is over, I think I'll be able to improve my grades.*
B *Good for you. Which subject do you need a better grade in?*

Sounds right p. 139

Lesson C Conversation strategies I'll drive.

1 Conversation strategy Making offers and promises

A Imagine you are planning a barbecue with friends. What things do you put on your "to-do" list?

B 4.28 Listen. What does Olivia offer to do? How about Jake?

Olivia I'm really looking forward to the barbecue this weekend.

Jake Me too. I'll get some steaks, if you like.

Olivia OK. That sounds good. And I'll bring some salad and stuff. Will you bring some chairs? Oh, and remind me to bring my beach umbrella.

Jake All right. And I won't forget the drinks this time, either.

Olivia Good. Uh, do you want me to drive?

Jake No, I'll drive. You can't afford any more speeding tickets.

Olivia OK. Then make sure you go to the gas station before you pick me up. We don't want to run out of gas again.

Jake All right. I will. But hey, we only ran out of gas that one time!

C Notice how Olivia and Jake use *I'll* and *I won't* to make offers and promises. Find examples in the conversation.

"I'll get some steaks." (an offer)
"I won't forget the drinks." (a promise)

D Some friends are planning a hiking trip for Saturday. For each comment, find and complete an offer or a promise with *I'll* or *I won't*. Then practice with a partner.

1. How are we going to get there? __b__
2. Do we have to leave early? I might oversleep. ____
3. What food should we take? ____
4. How about something to drink, too? ____
5. Will you remember to bring your GPS? ____
6. Should we check the weather before we go? ____
7. Do we have a trail map? ____

a. Don't worry, ____ call you.
b. I can borrow my parents' car. __I'll__ drive.
c. No, we don't. ____ get one.
d. Just some sandwiches. ____ make them.
e. Probably. ____ look at the forecast.
f. Sure. ____ forget. ____ bring a camera, too.
g. Yeah. ____ buy some bottles of water later.

About you **E** **Pair work** Imagine you are going on a day trip. Choose a place to go. Then take turns asking and answering the questions above. Make offers and promises with *I'll* and *I won't*.

2 Strategy plus *All right* and *OK*

You can use *All right* or *OK* when you agree to something.

In conversation

OK is about six times more frequent than *All right*.

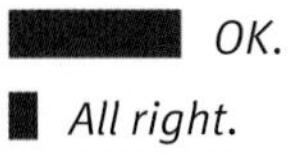

Respond to the questions with *All right* or *OK*, and make an offer with *I'll*. Then practice with a partner.

1. A Could you help me with my computer? I think it has a virus.
   B ________ . I'll ______________________________ .
2. A I have a favor to ask. Can you give me a ride to class tomorrow?
   B ________ . I'll ______________________________ .
3. A I might get a new tablet this weekend. Can you help me choose one?
   B ________ . I'll ______________________________ .
4. A I'm going to paint my apartment next weekend. Could you help me?
   B ________ . I'll ______________________________ .

A *Could you help me with my computer? I think it has a virus.*
B *All right. I'll take a look this afternoon. Is that OK?*

3 Listening and strategies I'll do it!

A 4.29 **Listen to Jack and Helen's conversation. What kind of event are they planning? Where will it take place? When?**

B 4.29 **Listen again. Complete the sentences. Write *a* to *h*. There is one extra item.**

1. Their mother promises she'll _____ and _____ .
2. Jack says he'll _____ . He says he won't _____ .
3. Helen says she'll _____ . She won't _____ . Helen will also _____ .

a. burn the food	d. send invitations online	g. shop and do the cooking
b. buy a gift and a card	e. get the date wrong	h. pay for everything
c. send a guest list	f. choose the music	

C **Group work** **Plan an end-of-the-year event for your class. Make a list of things to do. Offer and agree to do the different tasks.**

A *We should reserve a room at the school.*
B *OK, I'll call and do that.*
C *And we need to buy some snacks. . . .*

TO DO
Reserve a room at the school.
Buy some snacks.

In the future . . .

1 Reading

A Look at the pictures in the article. Can you guess what inventions the article will describe? Tell the class.

"I think people will use special glasses to get directions."

B Read the article. Which inventions did you already know about? Which were new?

Reading tip

As you read, look for words like *however*, which shows a contrasting idea, and *so*, which sometimes introduces a consequence.

http://www.lifeinthefuture...

WHAT WILL LIFE BE LIKE IN THE FUTURE?

Our analyst says that some weird and wonderful ideas of the future might not be that far away.

1 Smartphones, tablets, and laptops are getting thinner and lighter than ever before. However, in the future, you might not need to carry any gadgets around with you. If designers have their way, you may just need to wear a pair of "virtual goggles" instead. Scientists are testing prototypes at the moment, though it may be some time before they're actually on store shelves. These goggles will act like a computer screen and display information and entertainment from the Internet.

So, when you are sightseeing, you'll be able to see information about a famous building in front of you. Or you'll be able to get a review of the restaurant menu you're looking at. The goggles will have GPS, so you'll be able to stream directions to a party or locate a nearby coffee shop. They will also have a camera to take photos, and you won't need a cell phone anymore. The goggles will have that built in, too.

2 You might not be able to take a trip into space right now, but in the near future, we may all have access to the outer atmosphere. Private spaceships are taking reservations – at a cost – for flights into space. In the meantime, a Japanese company says it is developing a space elevator. The elevator, which will carry 30 passengers, will stretch from a base on the ground up to a space station 36,000 kilometers (22,000 miles) above the earth. It will take eight days to reach the space station. Luckily, the elevator will have beds and entertainment on board. The company says it may be ready by 2050.

3 You can already buy mirrors with TVs in them, so you can watch the morning news while you brush your teeth. However, in the future, mirrors will be able to do much, much more. What would you look like with long blond hair? Or with a beard? In the future, you will be able to simply tap your mirror if you want to see yourself with different features. Your mirror will also monitor your health, and it'll be able to tell you when you need a visit to the doctor's office. And before you go to work, you'll be able to set the time for a nice, relaxing bath. Now how hot do you want the water?

C **Read the article again. Check (✓) the predictions the article makes.**

1. ☐ With "virtual goggles" you'll be able to go online.
2. ☐ These goggles will make it unnecessary for tourists to go sightseeing.
3. ☐ Virtual goggles will have built-in cell phones.
4. ☐ Only trained astronauts will be able to travel on the space elevator.
5. ☐ The space elevator will carry people 22,000 miles above the earth.
6. ☐ The space elevator will probably be ready in the next ten years.
7. ☐ A "smart mirror" will show us what we look like with different hair or features.
8. ☐ With smart mirrors to monitor health, we won't need to go to the doctor.

About you **D** **Pair work** **If the predictions are correct, will our lives be better or worse? Discuss with a partner.**

A ***Our lives will be worse with virtual goggles. We'll stop looking at things around us.***

B ***I don't really agree. People won't wear the goggles all the time. Just when they need them.***

2 Listening and writing A good idea?

A 4.30 **Listen to Sophia and Alan discuss the inventions from the article on page 124. For each invention, who says it's a good idea? Check (✓) Sophia or Alan.**

Invention	Who says it's a good idea?		Why?
	Sophia	Alan	
1. virtual goggles	☐	☐	______
2. a space elevator	☐	☐	______
3. a smart mirror	☐	☐	______

About you **B** 4.30 **Listen again. Write *one* reason why Sophia or Alan thinks the invention is a good idea. Do you agree? Discuss with a partner.**

C **Read the article below and the Help note. Underline the words that list ideas.**

Home | Edit | Document Elements | Tables | Table Layout | Charts | Smart Art

"Smart" Refrigerators

Scientists predict that people will have "smart" refrigerators in the future. Scanners will read bar codes on food and . . .

I think this will make our lives better. First, you won't need to go grocery shopping anymore, so . . . Second, you'll never come home and find an empty refrigerator . . . Next, scanners will tell you if the food is bad, so you won't get sick . . . Finally, you'll be able to . . .

Help note

Listing ideas

First, *you won't need to . . .*
Second, *you'll never . . .*
Next, *scanners will . . .*
Finally, *you'll be able to . . .*

About you **D** **Write a short article about a future invention. Will it make life better or worse? Why? Give four reasons.**

Free talk p. 135

Vocabulary notebook

Learning tip *Grouping vocabulary*

Write new vocabulary in groups. You can group words by their endings or by their meanings. You can group expressions by different topic areas.

In conversation

Talk about jobs

The jobs people mention most in conversation are ***lawyer***, ***teacher***, and ***doctor***.

1 **Look at these jobs. Group them by their endings. How many other jobs can you add to each list?**

✓actor	assistant	doctor	journalist	musician	police officer
architect	consultant	electrician	letter carrier	nurse	receptionist
artist	dentist	firefighter	librarian	paramedic	writer

-er / -or	-ant / -ent	-ist	-ian	other
actor				

2 **Make a chart like the one below. How many expressions can you write in the chart?**

Work	Home and family	Education
get a promotion	*have a baby*	*take an exam*

On your own

Make a list of 20 people you know. What jobs do they do? Write their jobs in English. How many new words do you learn?

Can Do! Now I can . . .

✓ I can . . . ? I need to review how to . . .

- ☐ discuss my plans and make predictions.
- ☐ talk about jobs.
- ☐ make offers and promises.
- ☐ agree to offers, requests, and suggestions.
- ☐ understand a conversation about planning events.
- ☐ understand a conversation about inventions.
- ☐ read an article about the future.
- ☐ write an article about a future invention.

1 Who's who?

Austin and Tyler are brothers, but they look very different. Complete the questions for items 1 to 5. Complete items 6 to 9 with comparatives and prepositions. Compare with a partner. Then ask and answer the questions.

1. A ____________ alike?
   B No, they look totally different.
2. A ____________ like?
   B He's short and heavy, and he's got a mustache.
3. A ____________ like – his mother or his father?
   B Austin looks like his mother. She's short, too.
4. A ____________ ?
   B He's six feet tall. He's a lot taller than Austin.
5. A ____________ ?
   B His eyes are blue.
6. A Do they both have brown hair?
   B Yes, but Tyler's hair is ________ and ________ than Austin's.
7. A Are they both muscular?
   B No, Austin is ________ than Tyler. He works out ________ than Tyler.
8. A Do they both have freckles?
   B Yes, but Tyler has ________ freckles than Austin. Austin probably spends ________ time in the sun.
9. A Is Tyler the one ________ the spiked hair?
   B No, that's Austin. Tyler's the one ________ the ponytail – the one ________ the striped shirt.

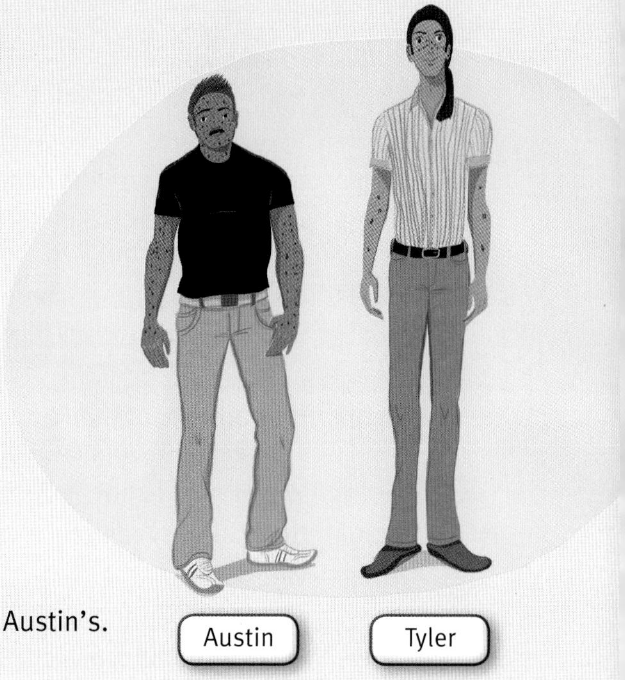

2 Can you guess what I mean?

A **How many words and expressions can you add to the chart? Compare charts with a partner.**

Describing faces	Describing hairstyles	Ways of communicating	Jobs
have freckles	*have a ponytail*	*text someone*	*electrician*

B **Pair work** **Student A: Explain a word or expression to a partner. Student B: Guess the word.**

A You can do this with your phone or computer.
B Do you mean text someone?

3 Can you complete this conversation?

Complete the conversation with the words and expressions in the box. Use capital letters where necessary. Practice with a partner. Then role-play the conversation using your own ideas.

all right	I'll	just	wearing	where were we
breaking up	I'll call you back	let's see	what do you call it	with
hold on a second	I've got	✓this is	what was I saying	you mean

Greg Greg Waters.

Kenji Hello, Greg. ___*This is*___ Kenji from the office in Tokyo. I was ____________ calling to ask . . . What time are you arriving on Monday?

Greg Well, I have my ticket here. ____________ , I arrive at, um, 3:30 p.m.

Kenji OK, ____________ come to the airport to meet you. Oh, ____________ – I've got another call.

Greg ____________ . . .

Kenji Hi. Sorry about that. So, ____________ ? Oh, yes, I'll meet you. So, how will I recognize you?

Greg Well, I'm tall and ____________ blond hair and –

Kenji Sorry, Greg, I can't hear you. You're ____________ .

Greg OK. Listen, ____________ . . .

Kenji Hi. That's better. So, ____________ ?

Greg I was describing myself. So, um, I'll be the blond guy ____________ the sunglasses, ____________ a USA T-shirt.

Kenji Um, OK. Maybe I should wear a – ____________ ? A thing with my name on it so you can find me?

Greg Oh, ____________ a badge. Good idea!

4 Future plans and dreams

A Circle the correct options, and then complete the sentences with true information.

1. When **I'll get** / **I get** home tonight, I'm going to ____________ , and I might ____________ , but I probably won't ____________ .
2. If **you'll want** / **you want** help with your homework this weekend, **I'll help** / **I help** you. I'm not ____________ on Saturday, but I may ____________ on Sunday.
3. If **I'll win** / **I win** the lottery this year, I promise **I'll buy** / **I buy** all my classmates dinner. I'll also ____________ , and I might ____________ , too.
4. If I ever **will become** / **become** famous, I **won't** / **don't** change. **I'll still be** / **I'm still** myself, and I won't ____________ .

B Pair work **Tell each other your sentences. Can you continue the conversations?**

UNIT 7 **Travel smart!**

1 Look at the pictures. What advice do you have for Traveler B in each situation? Make a list.

2 Role play Now imagine you and your partner are in the situations above. Take turns giving and responding to advice.

A *You know, maybe you shouldn't leave your money in your pocket like that.*

B *Oh, yeah, I guess. But I don't have a wallet.*

A *Why don't you go to that shop to look for a new wallet?*

UNIT 8 All about home

1 Pair work **Discuss the questions. Find three ways you're alike. Find three ways you're different.**

1. What's your room like at home?
   - What do you have on your walls?
   - Do you have a TV in your room?
   - Would you like to change your room? What would you change?
2. Are you neat or messy at home?
   - Do you make your bed every morning?
   - Do you leave things on top of dressers, tables, and chairs? Or do you put everything in drawers or a closet?
   - Is there a lot of clutter in your house? Whose clutter is it?

3. Do you prefer a quiet or a noisy home?
   - When you listen to music, do you use headphones or speakers?
   - Do you sing along with the music?
   - Do you leave the TV on when you're not watching?
4. Do you or your family do a "spring cleaning" every year?
   - Who does most of the work?
   - What do you do?
5. Do you have any unusual habits at home?

2 Group work **Join another pair. Tell them about yourself and your partner.**

"Mario and I both have small rooms, but he has posters of his favorite rock band on the wall. I just have some pictures of my friends and family on my desk."

Free talk

UNIT 9A What was happening?

Pair work Look at the picture. Bob just crashed into a lamppost. Some other people saw the accident. What were they doing when it happened? What was Bob doing? Study the picture and try to remember as many details as possible. Then turn to Free talk 9B on page 136.

UNIT 10 Which is better?

Pair work What are the advantages and disadvantages of the choices below? Which is better? Give at least three reasons for each choice. Discuss with your partner.

1. Is it better to own a motorcycle or a car?

2. Is it better to live in a small house or a big apartment?

3. Is it nicer to see a movie on your TV or on a big screen in a movie theater?

4. Is it more fun to take a vacation at the beach or in the city?

5. Which is worse – to have no Internet access or to have no TV?

A *Well, I think it's better to own a motorcycle than a car – and it's more fun.*
B *Actually, I agree. It's also easier to find parking spaces when you have a motorcycle.*
A *And it's just cheaper. Cars use more gas.*

UNIT 11A What's different?

Pair work Student A: These people are at the mall on Saturday morning. Your partner has a picture of the same people on Saturday afternoon. In that picture, each person is different in two ways. Ask questions to find out what's different. Where did each person go?

A *Do you see the woman with the dark hair?*
B *Yes. Is she wearing a blue dress in your picture?*
A *Yes, she is. So that's the same. Does she have a ponytail in your picture?*
B *No, she doesn't. Her hair is short. So that's different.*
A *I guess she went to the hair salon.*

UNIT 12 I might do that.

Pair work Write your answers to the questions in the chart. Then compare answers with a partner. Ask questions to find out more information and continue the conversations.

Can you think of . . .	My answers
1. something you may do when you get home tonight?	
2. someone you'll probably see next week?	
3. something you might do next year?	
4. something new you'd like to try?	
5. a place you might visit in the next five years?	
6. something you think you'll do if you earn a lot of money?	
7. something you might do when you retire?	
8. something you'll probably never do in your life?	

A *OK. So, I may cook myself a nice dinner tonight if I'm not too tired.*
B *Nice. What do you think you'll cook?*
A *Oh, maybe some pasta or something.*
B *I have a great recipe for pasta. I'll find it for you.*
A *All right. Thanks.*

UNIT 9B What was happening?

1 Pair work How much do you remember about the picture in Free talk 9A on page 134? Discuss the questions with a partner. Do you agree on the answers?

1. What was Bob doing when he crashed? What did he crash into?
2. What else was he doing?
3. What color were his sneakers?
4. What else was he wearing?
5. Was he wearing a helmet?
6. How many people saw the accident?
7. What was the young boy holding in his hand?
8. What happened when the boy saw the accident?
9. What was the man at the flower shop doing?
10. What was the man wearing? What did he shout?
11. What were the girls in the café doing when Bob hit the lamppost?
12. What were the girls wearing?
13. What was the woman in front of the grocery store carrying?
14. What did she do when Bob passed her?
15. How many other details can you remember?

A *I think he was riding a scooter.*
B *Actually, I'm pretty sure he was riding a skateboard. OK. What did he crash into?*

2 Pair work Now look at the picture in Free talk 9A again to check your answers. How many did you get right?

UNIT 11B What's different?

Pair work Student B: These people are at the mall on Saturday afternoon. Your partner has a picture of the same people on Saturday morning. In that picture, each person is different in two ways. Ask questions to find out what's different. Where did each person go?

A *Do you see the woman with the dark hair?*
B *Yes. Is she wearing a blue dress in your picture?*
A *Yes, she is. So that's the same. Does she have a ponytail in your picture?*
B *No, she doesn't. Her hair is short. So that's different.*
A *I guess she went to the hair salon.*

Sounds right

UNIT 7

4.37 **Listen and repeat the words. Check (✓) the words that have a silent letter *l*.**

1. ☑ could
2. ☐ help
3. ☐ milk
4. ☐ old
5. ☐ salmon
6. ☐ should
7. ☐ silk
8. ☐ talk
9. ☐ walk
10. ☐ would

UNIT 8

4.38 **Listen and repeat the words. Notice the underlined sounds. Match the words with the same underlined sounds.**

1. jewelry *e*
2. nightstand ____
3. oven ____
4. shower ____
5. sofa ____

a. microwave
b. round
c. stove
d. stuff
e. suit

UNIT 9

4.39 **Listen and repeat the sentences. Notice the underlined sounds. Check (✓) the verbs that have an extra syllable and end in /ɪd/.**

1. ☐ I called for help.
2. ☐ I sprained my wrist.
3. ☐ I deleted my photos.
4. ☐ I damaged the car.
5. ☐ It happened last week.
6. ☐ I waited an hour.

UNIT 10

4.40 **Listen and repeat the words. Notice the underlined sounds. Are the sounds like the sound in *see* or *zero*? Write *s* or *z*.**

1. always __z__
2. busy ____
3. business ____
4. calls ____
5. concert ____
6. easier ____
7. expensive ____
8. less ____
9. message ____
10. nicer ____
11. spam ____
12. worse ____

UNIT 11

4.41 **Listen and repeat the words. Notice the underlined sounds. Match the words with the same underlined sounds.**

1. cornrows ____
2. freckles ____
3. mustache ____
4. shaved ____
5. pierced ____
6. wear ____
7. blouse ____

a. beard
b. braids
c. hair
d. brown
e. head
f. muscular
g. short

UNIT 12

4.42 **Listen and repeat the words. Notice that some syllables are weak like the /ə/ sound in *away* or the /ər/ sound in *dinner*. Other syllables are strong, like the syllable *sis* in *assistant*. Circle the stressed (strongest) syllable.**

1. as(sis)tant
2. carrier
3. doctor
4. journalist
5. letter
6. officer
7. paramedic
8. promotion
9. police
10. representative

UNIT 7

Lesson A Infinitives for reasons; *It's* + adjective + *to* . . .

A Correct the conversations. Pay attention to infinitives for reasons and *It's / Is it* + adjective + *to*.

1. A Do you ever go online *to* buy train or bus tickets?
   B Well, I buy train tickets online because expensive buy them at the train station.
2. A Do you use a credit card or a debit card pay for things online?
   B A debit card. I'm only 17, and is just not possible get a credit card at my age.
3. A Do you have to travel far visit your family?
   B Well, my grandparents live about three hours away. So we take the bus go and see them. It's a long trip, but that's OK. I think is important see your family.
4. A Do you think it's fun travel alone?
   B It depends. I guess it nice have a friend with you when you go sightseeing.
5. A Is easy to get around in your town?
   B It's pretty easy. You can take the subway get to most places. It's fast and cheap.
6. A What do you do on the weekends relax?
   B I like to go to the beach go windsurfing.

About you **B Write your own answers to the questions. Then ask and answer the questions with a partner.**

UNIT 7

Lesson B Advice and suggestions

> **Common errors**
>
> Do not leave out *to* after *need*.
>
> *You **need to take** a toothbrush.*
> (NOT *You ~~need take a . . .~~*)

A Circle the correct words to complete the conversations. Then compare with a partner. Do you agree with the advice?

1. A I have to fly on Friday, but I have a cold. What **I should / should I** do?
   B Well, you probably shouldn't **go / to go** to work. Just **stay / staying** home and don't **go / to go** out. And don't forget **take / to take** some cold medicine on the plane with you.
2. A I'm going camping next weekend. Should I **take / to take** insect repellent?
   B Oh, you definitely need **have / to have** some this time of year. It's probably **good idea / a good idea** to take some shirts with long sleeves, too. And why **don't you / you don't** take something for bites in your first-aid kit?
3. A We're going to the beach next weekend. What **need / should** I take with me?
   B Well, you should **take / taking** an umbrella. It gets hot. And you probably need **pack / to pack** a picnic. The cafés are expensive. And **do you want / do you want to** take a volleyball? It's fun to play volleyball on the beach.

About you **B Pair work Write two of your own suggestions for each question above. Take turns asking the questions and making suggestions.**

UNIT 8 Lesson A *Whose . . . ?*; Possessive pronouns

Complete the questions with *whose* and a verb. Then complete the conversation with possessive pronouns. Practice with a partner.

1. Teacher I can hear a cell phone! Uh, ___whose___ phone ___is___ it?
   Student Oh, I'm really sorry. It's ___mine___ . . . . Sorry. I just turned it off.
2. Teacher I think someone left a backpack. ________ backpack ________ under that chair?
   Student Um, Mario has a backpack like that. I think it's ________ .
3. Teacher Two people forgot to write their names on the test. ________ tests ________ these?
   Student Let's see. That looks like Angela's handwriting. It's probably ________ . Oh, and that's ________ . Sorry I forgot to put my name on it.
4. Teacher I found these glasses last week after class. ________ glasses ________ they?
   Student Well, Manuel usually wears glasses in class. Maybe they're ________ .
   Teacher Excuse me, Manuel. I think these are ________ .
5. Teacher ________ science project ________ this? Does anyone know?
   Student Oh, it's Dana and Pam's. Well, I *think* it's ________ .

UNIT 8 Lesson B Order of adjectives; pronouns *one* and *ones*

Complete these conversations with the pronouns *one* or *ones*. Unscramble the last sentences. Then practice with a partner.

> **Common errors**
>
> Use *one* for a singular noun and *ones* for a plural noun.
>
> *I want to buy a new cell phone. Which **one** should I get?*
> (NOT *Which ~~ones~~ should I get?*)

1. A I need to buy a new water bottle. Should I buy a plastic ________ or a metal ________ ?
   B You can get some really cool ________ . get / You / metal / nice / should / a / one
   ____ .
2. A I think shoes are expensive. Maybe because I always buy expensive leather ________ .
   B I know a great discount store. shoes / leather / buy / inexpensive / You / can / there
   ____ .
3. A You needed a new tablet cover, right? Did you find a nice ________ ?
   B Uh-huh. red / one / found / plastic / I / a / pretty
   ____ .
4. A I need new pants for the winter. Which ________ should I buy? Some wool pants or those cotton ________ ?
   B Well, wool is nice. get / You / some / pants / should / wool / black
   ____ .
5. A What kind of rug did you buy for your bedroom? A Turkish ________ ?
   B Actually, I decided to buy something different. beautiful / I / a / Indian / rug / bought / little
   ____ .

UNIT 9
Lesson A Past continuous statements

A Complete the sentences with the past continuous or the simple past. Compare with a partner.

1. I was in class last week, and the teacher *was explaining* (explain) something, and I just *fell* (fall) asleep. When I __________ (wake up), I realized that everyone __________ (look) at me.
2. Yesterday I __________ (walk) down the street, and I __________ (text) a friend when I __________ (walk) right into a lamppost. I guess I __________ (not pay) attention.
3. My sister and her husband __________ (carry) some dishes into the kitchen when they both __________ (trip) over a rug. They __________ (drop) and __________ (break) all their new dishes!
4. Last week a friend of mine __________ (invite) me over for dinner. In the afternoon, when she __________ (cook), she __________ (pick up) a heavy pot and __________ (hurt) her back. When I __________ (arrive), she __________ (lie) on the sofa, so I __________ (make) dinner for us!
5. The other day, a friend and I were at my house. We __________ (not / do) anything special, so I __________ (say), "Come on. Let's go out for coffee. It's on me." While I __________ (wait) in line to order, I __________ (realize) I didn't have my wallet. So my friend __________ (pay) for everything. I was really embarrassed.

About you **B Choose two of the situations above and rewrite them with your own information.**

I was in class last week, and my friend was sending a text when the teacher asked him a question.

UNIT 9
Lesson B Past continuous questions; reflexive pronouns

A Complete the questions in the conversations and add reflexive pronouns. Practice with a partner.

1. A I accidentally burned *myself* when I was cooking dinner.
   B Oh, no! What *were you making* (make)?
   A I was making a vegetable curry.
2. A My sister hurt __________ at the gym last night. She sprained her ankle.
   B That's too bad. __________ (do) aerobics?
   A No, she was doing yoga. I guess you can hurt __________ if you're not careful.
3. A Was there anyone fun at the party last night? I mean, who __________ (talk) to?
   B Oh, this really boring guy. He talked about __________ the whole time. I didn't talk about __________ once!
4. A When I got home last night, my kids were arguing.
   B Really? What __________ (fight) about?
   A Who should do the dishes. I just can't leave them by __________ .
5. A There was a lot of noise when I called you last night. What __________ (do)?
   B Last night? I was having dinner with some friends at a restaurant. We were really enjoying __________ .

Common errors

Use the past continuous, not the simple past, for longer actions.

*When I **was making** dinner, a friend called.*
(NOT *When I ~~made~~ dinner, a friend called.*)

About you **B Pair work Think of situations like the ones above. Tell a partner what happened.**

"I accidentally burned myself when I was camping last summer."

UNIT 10 Lesson A Comparative adjectives

A Complete these questions with the comparative forms of the adjectives (↑ = more; ↓ = less). Compare with a partner. Then write an answer for each question.

In your opinion . . .

1. Which is *less expensive* (expensive ↓), an e-reader or a tablet?
   An e-reader is less expensive than a tablet, but a tablet is more useful.
2. Is it ____________ (easy ↑) to read an e-book or a regular book outside?
   ____
3. Which is ____________ (useful ↑), a cell phone or a tablet?
   ____
4. Is it ____________ (difficult ↓) to write an email on a laptop or on a smartphone?
   ____
5. Which is ____________ (nice ↑) for personal messages, email or a social network?
   ____
6. Is it ____________ (bad ↑) to lose your laptop or your phone?
   ____
7. Is it ____________ (good ↑) to hold your cell phone or use an earpiece when you call someone?
   ____
8. Why are phone calls becoming ____________ (popular ↓) than text messages?
   ____

About you **B Pair work** **Take turns asking and answering the questions. Give reasons for your opinions.**

UNIT 10 Lesson B *More, less, fewer*

Common errors

Use *than* after a comparative, not *that* or *then*.

Texting is quicker **than** *calling.*
(NOT *Texting is quicker* ~~*that*~~ *calling.*)

A Complete the sentences with *more*, *less*, or *fewer*. Then compare with a partner.

1. I'm spending *less* time on my social network these days because I'm very busy at work.
2. I'm getting ________ exercise now because I'm walking home from work every day.
3. My friends and I text each other very late at night, so I'm sleeping ________ than I should.
4. My friends prefer texting to email, so they're sending me ________ email messages these days.
5. I don't have much time to cook, so I'm eating out ________ than I did before.
6. I don't like big groups. I enjoy myself ________ when I have dinner with just one or two close friends.
7. I feel a bit shy in groups. I usually talk ________ than other people.
8. In my family, we're watching TV ________ together because we're all spending more and more time on our laptops.
9. I'm buying ________ newspapers now because I'm getting my news online.

About you **B Pair work** **Are the sentences above true for you? Discuss with your partner.**

"I think I'm spending more time on my social network these days. I have more and more friends – around 500 now."

Extra practice

UNIT 11 **Lesson A** Describing people; *have got*

Common errors

Do not use *look like* before an adjective.

*He **looks** tired.*
(NOT *He ~~looks like~~ tired.*)

About you **Write questions for the answers. Practice with a partner. Then ask and answer the questions, giving your own information.**

1. A ______________________, your mother or your father?
   B I think I look more like my mother.
2. A ______________________________________?
   B My father's hair is dark brown.
3. A ______________________________________?
   B No, she doesn't. She's got very straight hair.
4. A ______________________________________?
   B My mother? She's about one meter seventy-five (five foot seven).
5. A ______________________________________?
   B My best friend? He's tall and thin, and he's got curly black hair.
6. A ______________________________________?
   B No, we don't look alike. My friend is a lot taller than I am.

UNIT 11 **Lesson B** Phrases with the verb + *-ing* and prepositions

A Someone is asking questions about the people in the photo. Unscramble the sentences. Label the people. Then practice with a partner.

1. A the / with / the / blond hair / tall / who's / guy
   ______________________________________?
   B That's Adrian. He's about six foot four.
2. A woman / who's / standing / the / him / next to
   ______________________________________?
   B Angela. She's in my math class.
3. A wearing / the / woman / yellow / the / top / blond / who's
   ______________________________________?
   B That's Abby. She's a good friend of Daniel's.
4. A Daniel? Is he in the picture?
   B Yeah. the / he's / shaved head / guy / with / the
   ______________________________________?
5. A Is your friend Gina in the picture? Which one is she?
   B top / the / in / she's / orange / woman / the
   ______________________________________?

_____ _____ _____ _____ _____

B Pair work **Ask and answer questions about the people in the photo.**

"Which one is Adrian?" *"Who's the woman wearing the orange top?"*

UNIT 12 Lesson A Future with *will*, *may*, and *might*

A Read the questions about future plans and choose the best options in the answers. Then practice with a partner.

1. A Are you going to the beach on Saturday?
   B Probably not. It looks like **it'll rain** / **it rains** all weekend.
2. A Do you have plans to move to a new apartment?
   B Actually, **I'll move** / **I'm moving** next week – I just found a new place!
3. A Are you going to take another English course next semester?
   B I'm not sure. **I might not** / **I won't** have enough time.
4. A How are you going to celebrate your next birthday?
   B Well, **I'll be** / **I may be** 30 on my next birthday, but I don't think **I'll** / **I may** do anything special.
5. A Do you think you'll travel abroad in the next couple of years?
   B I don't know. Maybe **I'll go** / **I go** to Spain to learn Spanish.
6. A Do you think you'll be rich someday?
   B No. I know **I won't** / **I may not** be rich because I'm not very good with money.

Common errors

Don't use the simple present instead of *will* + verb for predictions.

I don't think it ***will rain.***
(NOT *I don't think it* ~~*rains*~~.)

About you **B Pair work Ask and answer the questions. Give your own information.**

UNIT 12 Lesson B Present tense verbs with future meaning

A Choose the best expressions to complete these questions. Then compare with a partner.

1. Are you going to do anything interesting after class **will be** / **is** over today?
2. After you **will eat** / **eat** dinner tonight, are you going to do any work?
3. What do you think **you'll do** / **you do** before you go to bed tonight?
4. If you **don't** / **won't** fall asleep right away, do you think you'll read for a while?
5. What's the first thing you're going to do when **you'll get up** / **you get up** tomorrow morning?
6. Are you going to exercise tomorrow before **you'll have** / **you have** breakfast?
7. If it **doesn't** / **won't** rain tomorrow, do you think you'll go running or go for a walk?
8. Are you going to meet your friends tomorrow when you **get out** / **will get out** of class?
9. If you **don't** / **won't** have time to eat breakfast at home tomorrow, will you have an early lunch?
10. If you **will go out** / **go out** this weekend, where will you go?

Common errors

Don't use *will* after *if*, *when*, *before*, and *after* to refer to the future.

When I ***graduate****, I'll look for a job.*
(NOT *When I* ~~*will graduate*~~*, I'll look for a job.*)

About you **B Pair work Ask and answer the questions. What do you have in common?**

Illustration credits

Harry Briggs: 27, 79, 95, 100, 101, 134 **Bunky Hurter:** 10, 20, 30, 42, 52, 62 *(bottom)*, 74, 84, 94, 106, 116, 126 **Cambridge University Press:** 47 *(bottom left border)*, 55, 66 *(top right)*, 94 *(top)* **Kim Johnson:** 25, 81, 91, 128, 132 **Scott Macneil:** 18, 54, 56, 60, 62 *(top)*, 145 **Frank Montagna:** 28, 124, 135, 136 **Q2A studio artists:** 69, 86, 111, 120 **Gavin Reece:** 31, 87, 103, 121 **Lucy Truman:** 4, 89, 96, 108, 127

Photography credits

Back cover: ©vovan/Shutterstock **16, 17, 58, 59, 80, 90, 91, 102, 103, 122, 123** ©Cambridge University Press **6, 7, 26, 27, 34, 38, 39, 44, 48, 49, 70, 71, 76, 112, 113** ©Frank Veronsky **viii** *(left)* ©Rich Legg/Getty Images/RF; *(right)* ©Image Source/SuperStock **1** *(clockwise from top left)* ©Corbis/SuperStock; ©Asia Images/SuperStock; ©Jesse Wild/Total Guitar magazine/Getty Images; ©Thinkstock **2** ©AsiaPix/SuperStock **3** ©Thinkstock **5** *(left to right)* ©Blue Jean Images/SuperStock; *(tv)* ©Pakhnyushcha/Shutterstock; *(news)* ©Heather Wines/CBS via Getty Images; ©Flirt/SuperStock; ©GoodMood Photo/istockphoto **7** *(bottom)* ©kristian sekulic/istockphoto **8** *(left)* ©Steve Debenport/istockphoto; *(right)* ©Thinkstock **9** ©Chris Pecoraro/istockphoto **11** *(top row, left to right)* ©photovideostock/istockphoto; ©Nadya Lukic/istockphoto; ©YinYang/istockphoto *(bottom row, left to right)* ©Alberto Pomares/istockphoto; ©Ken Babione/istockphoto; ©Thinkstock; *(tablet)* ©L_amica/Shutterstock **12** ©Don Bayley/Getty Images/RF; *(background)* ©Feng Yu/Shutterstock **14** *(top row, left to right)* ©Kevin Mazur/WireImage/Getty Images; ©Kevin Mazur/WireImage/Getty Images; ©George Pimentel/WireImage/Getty Images; ©Lucas Jackson/Reuters/Corbis *(bottom row, left to right)* ©Handout/WireImage/Getty Images; ©Roberta Parkin/Redferns via Getty Images; ©David Redfern/Redferns/Getty Images; ©TIZIANA FABI/AFP/Getty Images **15** ©Dougal Waters Photography Ltd/Getty Images/RF **17** *(bottom, left to right)* ©Casey McNamara/Getty Images; ©Charlie Neuman/ZUMA Press/Corbis; ©Exactostock/SuperStock; ©Thomas Trötscher/istockphoto **18** *(top to bottom)* ©Tyler Olson/Shutterstock; ©nimu1956/istockphoto **19** ©Ridofranz/istockphoto **21** *(clockwise from top left)* ©Alex Brosa/Getty Images; ©Design Pics/SuperStock; ©Chris Schmidt/Getty Images; ©Belinda Images/SuperStock; ©Nicolas McComber/istockphoto; ©Cultura Limited/SuperStock **22** *(top row, left to right)* ©Jamie Carroll/istockphoto; ©Fotolia; ©Thinkstock *(bottom row, left to right)* ©digitalskillet/istockphoto; ©Thinkstock; ©Asia Images/SuperStock; *(background)* ©Natutik/Shutterstock **23** ©Elena Ray/Shutterstock **24** *(top row, left to right)* ©age fotostock/SuperStock; ©B BOISSONNET/BSIP/SuperStock; ©MAY/BSIP/SuperStock; ©laflor/istockphoto *(bottom row, left to right)* ©Blend Images/SuperStock; ©Jens Koenig/Getty Images; ©flyfloor/Getty Images; ©Science Photo Library/SuperStock **25** ©DEX IMAGE/Getty Images/RF **29** *(top row, left to right)* ©Thinkstock; ©Thinkstock; ©age fotostock/SuperStock; ©Alexander Fortelny/istockphoto; *(middle, all photos)* ©Thinkstock; *(bottom, left to right)* ©Thinkstock; ©Silvia Jansen/istockphoto **33** *(clockwise from top left)* ©Thinkstock; ©Image Source/Getty Images; ©SuperStock; ©Cultura Limited/SuperStock; ©Andres Rodriguez/SuperFusion/SuperStock; ©Cusp/SuperStock **35** ©age fotostock/SuperStock **36** *(top row, left to right)* ©Thinkstock; ©Donna Coleman/istockphoto; ©Blue Jean Images/SuperStock *(bottom row, left to right)* ©bikeriderlondon/Shutterstock; ©Exactostock/SuperStock; ©Burke/Triolo Productions/Getty Images **37** ©hanibaram/istockphoto **39** *(bottom, left to right)* ©Charlie Neuman/ZUMA Press/Corbis; ©Christophe Boisvieux/Corbis **40** *(left to right)* ©AP Photo/Larry Crowe; ©Benjamin Loo/istockphoto; ©Jupiterimages/Getty Images/RF; *(background)* ©Paprika/Shutterstock **41** *(background)* ©Devor/Shutterstock **42** *(notebook background)* ©Elena Schweitzer/Shutterstock **43** *(clockwise from top left)* ©age fotostock/SuperStock; ©LEMOINE/BSIP/SuperStock; ©Blend Images/SuperStock; ©Fancy Collection/SuperStock **46** *(top row, left to right)* ©Nancy Louie/istockphoto; ©Fancy Collection/SuperStock; *(bottom row, left to right)* ©Juanmonino/istockphoto; ©Fancy Collection/SuperStock **47** *(top row, left to right)* ©Picsfive/Shutterstock; © dafne/Shutterstock; ©Thinkstock *(bottom row, left to right)* ©hh5800/istockphoto; ©Christopher Futcher/istockphoto; ©Thinkstock **49** *(bottom)* ©Cusp/SuperStock **50** ©Ron Levine/Getty Images **51** ©Thinkstock **53** *(clockwise from top right)* ©Jupiterimages/Thinkstock; ©Exactostock/SuperStock; ©age fotostock/SuperStock; ©Henry Westheim Photography/Alamy **57** ©Thinkstock **59** *(bottom)* ©Ivan Solis/istockphoto **60** *(top to bottom)* ©Thinkstock; ©Reimar Gaertner/age fotostock/SuperStock; *(background)* ©Thinkstock **61** *(top to bottom)* ©GUIZIOU Franck/hemi/Hemis.fr/SuperStock; ©freesoulproduction/Shutterstock **63** ©imagebroker.net/SuperStock **65** *(clockwise from top left)* ©Glow Images - 40260.com/SuperStock; ©Thomas Sztanek/Purestock/SuperStock; ©Fancy Collection/SuperStock; ©Maskot/Getty Images **66** ©Wendy Carter/istockphoto **67** ©Beyond/SuperStock **68** *(bathing suit)* ©sagir/Shutterstock; *(sandals)* ©Shevel Artur/Shutterstock; *(towel)* ©Mike Flippo/Shutterstock; *(cooler)* ©Danny E Hooks/Shutterstock; *(hat)* ©windu/Shutterstock; *(mp3 player)* ©Thinkstock; *(sunglasses)* ©Uros Zunic/Shutterstock; *(insect repellent)* ©andrea crisante/Shutterstock; *(tent)* ©trekandshoot/Shutterstock; *(GPS)* ©Thinkstock; *(camera)* ©Chiyacat/Shutterstock; *(scissors)* ©Phakkaphon Juawanich/Shutterstock; *(sleeping bag)* ©Mark Herreid/Shutterstock; *(first-aid kit)* ©Alan Crawford/istockphoto; *(pajamas)* ©Suljo/istockphoto; *(tablet computer)* ©Sashkin/Shutterstock; *(flashlight)* ©Artur Marfin/Shutterstock; *(batteries)* ©grekoff/Shutterstock; *(charger)* ©zirconicusso/Shutterstock; *(e-reader)* ©Ziva_K/istockphoto; *(brush)* ©FomaA/Shutterstock; *(hair dryer)* ©Nordling/Shutterstock; *(makeup)* ©Sergiy Kuzmin/Shutterstock; *(shampoo)* ©Alex011973/Shutterstock; *(soap)* ©Robert Red/Shutterstock; *(razor)* ©Lusoimages/Shutterstock; *(toothpaste)* ©Kenneth C. Zirkel/istockphoto; *(toothbrush)* ©George Dolgikh/Shutterstock; *(sunscreen)* ©Africa Studio/Shutterstock **71** *(bottom)* ©Exactostock/SuperStock **72** *(top to bottom)* ©Fotostudio Jaap Woets; ©EcoCamp Patagonia; ©The Safari Collection; *(tablet)* ©L_amica/Shutterstock **73** *(top row, left to right)* ©Hugh Rooney/Eye Ubiquitous/Corbis; ©Derek Croucher/Getty Images; ©imagebroker.net/SuperStock *(bottom)* ©Fotolia; *(background)* ©Nik Merkulov/Shutterstock **75** *(clockwise from top right)* ©Lisa F. Young/istockphoto; ©Digital Vision/Thinkstock; ©Lucas Allen/Corbis; ©Sheltered Images/SuperStock **77** ©peepo/istockphoto **78** (clockwise from top left) ©Thinkstock; ©Thinkstock; ©Frank Short/Istockphoto; ©Elena Elisseeva/Shutterstock **82** ©Don Farrall/Getty Images **83** *(top row, left to right)* ©Hans Laubel/istockphoto; *(news)* ©John Paul Filo/CBS vis Getty Images; ©George Doyle/Thinkstock; ©Tatyana Nyshko/istockphoto; ©RelaXimages/SuperStock; *(bottom row, left to right)* ©moodboard/SuperStock; ©Stephen Chiang/Getty Images; ©Image Source/SuperStock; ©Artazum/Shutterstock **84** *(left to right)* ©Ramsey Blacklock/istockphoto; ©ShutterWorx/istockphoto; ©Sawayasu Tsuji/istockphoto; ©Yenwen Lu/istockphoto **85** *(clockwise from top right)* ©Paula Connelly/istockphoto; ©Exactostock/SuperStock; ©Exactostock/SuperStock; ©Tom England/istockphoto **86** *(top to bottom)* ©Thinkstock; ©Thinkstock; ©Maria Teijeiro/Thinkstock **88** *(main photo)* ©Exactostock/SuperStock; *(top to bottom)* ©Kasiap/Shutterstock; ©Thinkstock; ©Thinkstock; ©Levent Konuk/Shutterstock; ©wavebreakmedia/Shutterstock **92** *(clockwise from top left)* ©Thinkstock; ©Thinkstock; ©Jupiterimages/Thinkstock; ©Stockbyte/Thinkstock **97** *(clockwise from top left)* ©Hocus Focus Studio/istockphoto; ©Exactostock/SuperStock; ©Radius/SuperStock; ©Blend Images/SuperStock; ©Exactostock/SuperStock; *(inset)* ©Shelly Perry/istockphoto **98** *(top row, left to right)* ©Jon Feingersh/MediaBakery; ©SZE FEI WONG/istockphoto; ©laflor/istockphoto; *(bottom row, left to right)* ©George Doyle/Thinkstock; *(inset)* ©Exactostock/SuperStock; ©BananaStock/Thinkstock **104** *(tablet)* ©L_amica/Shutterstock **107** ©Steve Debenport/istockphoto **110** *(top row, left to right)* ©Goldmund Lukic/istockphoto; ©Michael Bodmann/istockphoto; ©laflor/istockphoto; ©Fancy Collection/SuperStock; *(middle row, left to right)* ©Junko Yokoyama/Getty Images; ©Sanjay Deva/istockphoto; ©James Woodson/Thinkstock; ©Amos Morgan/Thinkstock; *(bottom row, left to right)* ©Jamie Choy/istockphoto; ©wrangel/istockphoto; ©Exactostock/SuperStock; ©Fancy Collection/SuperStock **112** *(bottom)* ©Jim Barber/Shutterstock **113** *(bottom, left to right)* ©vipflash/Shutterstock; ©Leonard Adam/Getty Images; ©Venturelli/Getty Images for P&G Prestige; ©Henry S. Dziekan III/Getty Images; ©s_bukley/Shutterstock; ©Francois Durand/Getty Images **114** *(top to bottom)* ©Thinkstock; ©selimaksan/istockphoto; ©Todd Smith istockphoto; ©AlexKol Photography/Shutterstock; ©coloroftime/istockphoto; ©sam100/Shutterstock; ©Radu Razvan/istockphoto **117** *(clockwise from top right)* ©Westend61/SuperStock; ©Westend61/SuperStock; ©Fancy Collection/SuperStock; ©Ocean/Corbis **118** *(clockwise from top right)* ©Christopher Futcher/istockphoto; ©Thinkstock; ©Juergen Bosse/istockphoto; ©Thinkstock; ©YinYang/istockphoto **123** *(bottom)* ©Yong Hian Lim/istockphoto **124** *(background)* ©URRRA/Shutterstock **129** *(left to right)* ©Belinda Images/SuperStock; ©Thinkstock; ©YinYang/istockphoto **130** ©Elena Kalistratova/istockphoto **131** ©Aleksandrs Gorins/istockphoto **133** ©Oleg Zabielin/Shutterstock **134** *(top row, left to right)* ©ewg3D/istockphoto; ©Henrik Jonsson/istockphoto; ©Linda Johnsonbaugh/istockphoto; ©zveiger alexandre/istockphoto; ©DrGrounds/istockphoto; ©Rich Legg/istockphoto; *(bottom row, left to right)* ©Yulia Popkova/istockphoto; ©Jon Arnold/Jon Arnold Images/SuperStock; ©LEMOINE/BSIP/SuperStock; ©Stockbroker/SuperStock **150** ©michaeljung/Shutterstock

Text credits

While every effort has been made, it has not always been possible to identify the sources of all the materials used, or to trace the copyright holders. If any omissions are brought to our notice, we will be happy to include the appropriate acknowledgements on reprinting.

50 Interview used with permission of Joseph Hodgson.